New Father's SURVIVAL GUIDE

Devotions for the First Year of Parenthood

Dean Nelson

NEW FATHER'S SURVIVAL GUIDE
Devotions for the First Year of Parenthood

Copyright © 1994 Augsburg Fortress. All rights reserved. Except for brief quotations in critical articles or reviews, no part of this book may be reproduced in any manner without prior written permission from the publisher. Write to: Permissions, Augsburg Fortress, 426 S. Fifth St., Box 1209, Minneapolis, MN 55440.

Scripture quotations unless otherwise noted are from the New Revised Standard Version of the Bible, copyright © 1989 by the Division of Christian Education of the National Council of Churches of Christ in the United States of America. Used with permission.

Scripture quotations noted NEB are from the New English Bible © 1961, 1970 by the Delegates of the Oxford University Press and the Syndics of the Cambridge University Press. Reprinted by permission.

Interior design: The Book Company
Cover art and design: Jeff Tolbert

Library of Congress Cataloging-in-Publication Data.

Nelson, Dean, 1954–
New father's survival guide : devotions for the first year of parenting / Dean Nelson.
p. cm.
Includes bibliographical references.
ISBN 0-8066-2591-0 (alk. paper)
1. Fathers—Prayer-books and devotions—English. 2. Fatherhood—Religious aspects—Christianity. I. Title.
BV4529.N45 1994
242'.645—dc20 93-49451
CIP

The paper used in this publication meets the minimum requirements of American National Standard for Information Sciences—Permanence of Paper for Printed Library Materials, ANSI Z329.48-1984. ∞™

Manufactured in the U.S.A. AF 9-2591

98 97 96 95 94 1 2 3 4 5 6 7 8 9 10

To Blake and Vanessa,
who created a completely new being
when they made me their dad.

Contents

Acknowledgments

This collection of meditations is the result of my keeping a daily journal from the day we found out my wife and I were having a baby, to our baby's first birthday. My wife, Marcia, suggested it, and I am grateful to her for being a consistent provider of good ideas as well as a marvelous companion. I am also grateful to Rebecca Laird Christensen, a friend, colleague, and extraordinary editor, who encouraged and helped me broaden the journal into something that other fathers might find useful. I am also grateful to Sharon Marsh, the secretary in the journalism program at Point Loma Nazarene College where I teach, for all of her extra work in making sure this manuscript was presentable.

The Faith of One Father

◆

[Abram] believed the LORD
and the LORD reckoned it to him
as righteousness.
Genesis 15:6

This is an age when practically any technological feat is possible. It is possible to know where Mars will be in the galaxy at a certain point on the calendar and to send a rocket from Earth weeks ahead of that point to get revealing pictures of the hot planet. On a simpler level, it is also possible to tell your computer at the office that you want your VCR at home to tape tonight's special six-hour "Mr. Ed" marathon. Anything is possible. Technology even makes it possible to plan when to become a father.

This was not Abraham's problem, of course. He wasn't waiting until he had his retirement accounts established, or until there was higher quality home-school curriculum, or until he could add another room to his tent before he wanted to be Father Abraham. God promised Abraham—at nearly one hundred years of age—that he would have a son who would be king over a great nation. Given Abraham's age and Sarah's ancient reproductive system (it's right there in Genesis 21), this was something beyond even present-day technological possibility. But then, a covenant with God overrules technology any day.

Even with the advances since Abraham's day, technology still can't do some things when it comes to fatherhood. It can't prepare you spiritually. It can't prepare you emotionally. It can't prepare you financially. There are books and classes, of course, that try to help couples anticipate what's ahead as they start to expand their families, yet all the information in the world can't really *prepare* a father-to-be.

Only becoming a dad can do that. The preparation is done on the run, with the new father depending on God for insight as each day arrives. It was true with Abraham, and it's still true.

My wife and I waited for nine years, trying to muster the courage to say we were ready spiritually, emotionally, and financially to become parents. We wanted to have some order in our lives before we disorganized them again. We wanted to have enough money in the bank. We kept saying, "Two more years, then we'll be ready." One of us was always in school and the other couldn't wait until that one got out so he or she could go back to school or find a different job.

On the one hand it seemed so right to have children. God has given most of us such an amazing chance to participate in creation that I was simultaneously nervous and excited about what he could produce out of my wife's and my genes. Our friends never stopped talking about their kids because they were so amazed by what God had created through them.

Still, we hesitated. It was clear from our friends' behavior that adding a baby to the family was an extremely joyous yet stressful experience. By having stable jobs and incomes, we felt that we could reduce some of the stress in advance.

Another hesitation was my own doubt about whether I could be an adequate dad. I don't know anyone who woke up one day and proclaimed, "Bring it on! I'm ready for fatherhood! Let's have the baby!" I had no formal training, no college degree for it. Just instinct and what I thought I remembered about what my own father did and didn't do right when I was young.

At what point is one ready to be a dad? I wanted to know in that area where deep calls to deep if I was equipped to be an adequate dad. Was I mature enough? Was my temper under control enough? Would I be a good enough role model? Would I be a reasonable representative of God the Father until the child could come to know God personally? It didn't seem possible.

These weren't life-style questions anymore. It wasn't a financial issue. And while I don't have much in common with Abraham (and, to set the record *entirely* straight, my wife has nothing in common with Sarah's dilemma), all potential fathers do have one point to share: becoming a father is a faith issue. Abraham had faith that God would make him a father. I saw my need for faith to become a good father. In a day when science and its resulting technology can grow a fertilized egg in a petri dish, chart a baby's development daily in the mother's womb, save a baby born several months prematurely, and provide a map of a baby's genetic makeup, nothing can predict how good a father a man will be.

Who, when faced with the question of adequacy, feels confident in advance about his parenting skills? What if we mess these kids up? Even if we avoid the obvious pitfalls like alcoholism, abuse, and long absences, what if we still don't get the job done?

Archie Bunker, that great theologian of the seventies, once said, "Faith is believing what no one else in his right mind would believe." And when anything involves faith, it involves risk. We're putting faith in a God we haven't seen, in an age when we can see practically everything.

I didn't talk about my fears with anyone. It sounded a little silly when the words started to form, because I hadn't heard anyone else talk about it. But the whole issue of being a good father made me uncertain. By faith Abraham settled in an alien land and believed God would provide for him and a generation to come. New fathers are headed for an alien land as well, needing the same kind of faith he had. Technology can't help us here. A child is God's creation, put under our responsibility. It is risky to think we will know what to do and say and be at the right time in the best interest of our new babies. "The LORD said to Abraham . . . Is anything too wonderful for the LORD?" (Gen. 18:14). God's rhetorical question presents us with a faith for all fathers.

Father in heaven, only you can provide the faith we need to continue in the direction you are leading us. Help me to depend less on technology and more on you as my father.

From Faith to Anticipation

◆

Faith is the assurance of things hoped for,
the conviction of things not seen.
Hebrews 11:1

There is something so exciting about the decision to expand a family that even those who normally respect your privacy turn into reporters for the grocery-store tabloids. That's the price you pay for telling *anyone* you and your wife hope to have a baby. The meaning of the word *secret* is different when it comes to babies. Normally, if a person says, "I'll keep it a secret," the person means "I'll tell no one, except maybe my spouse." The person can be trusted overall not to blab the information around.

Not so when it comes to babies. In this context, "I'll keep it a secret" really means "I'll only tell a few thousand of my very closest friends."

Once the word gets out (the time elapsed is approximately the same as that of a satellite signal reaching the earth), everyone will expect you to tell them as soon as you have conceived. Every telephone conversation will end with, "Do you have any exciting news for us?" As if you are going to talk about the umpire strike for thirty minutes before saying, "Oh, and by the way, we're going to have a baby." Every appointment you miss, people assume, is because you're taking a home pregnancy test.

My wife and I decided not to tell anyone about our new leap of faith. It's not that we didn't want to share the excitement; we didn't want to share the scrutiny. What if there was a miscarriage or other complication? Friends of ours told several people of their expansion plans, and when there was no public result after a couple of years, people started putting two and two together. There was a problem, of course. One former friend of theirs even called them forward during a church service so they could be "healed."

We didn't need that kind of pressure. As it turned out, fifteen months after deciding it was time to expand our family, we were still a family of two. What was wrong? We had faith, didn't we? God wasn't going to take my comparison to Abraham literally, was he?

I began noticing how many pregnant women there were in my office, church, and town. Thousands seemed to spring up around me, in the same way it seems everyone starts driving that one-of-a-kind car you want because it is so "different."

Visits with doctors to see if there was a fertility problem meant tests for both of us. The tests apparently unclogged something, because soon after those trips a baby was on the way.

The feeling that accompanies this knowledge is something new under the sun. It's not like the knowledge that the earth will maintain its orbit or that the Cleveland Indians will never win a World Series. Those are givens. Nor is it like the knowledge we have as Christians that Jesus loves us, that he is alive, and that he will return for us.

The knowledge that a baby is coming is a new creation all its own, a new mixture of excitement and terror. It means that things are going to change forever.

It is different from getting a new job where, if things don't work out, you can quit and look for another one. This is like marriage all over again, where you say you will accept the responsibility for life. But it's even more intense than marriage. A marriage is two reasonably grown-up people creating one shared life where there had previously been two. Having a baby is creating something where there had been nothing before. And it is largely up to you how this new creation will turn out. There is no test drive or probation period. There's no backing out. The baby is coming. Your influence has already begun and will never stop.

Knowing that a baby is coming is, in a sense, similar to accepting Christ. A new life is coming into existence, and you want to shout about it from the rooftops. But it's also such a private experience that you don't want to tell anyone. You just want to ponder it for a while and try to understand what it means. Suddenly you're different. Your wife is different. The world around you is different.

When do you tell? We let it be our secret for a week or so, then told our parents, who I assume kept the secret with only a dozen others. One by one, we told our closer friends, but within a few days people started calling us. The tabloids must have worked overtime that month.

The most memorable response to our news was from my grandmother, a spiritual giant, whose idea of fasting and praying is taking the cherry off her hot fudge sundae before she asks the blessing. She gave me the same response as when I told her I was getting married: "It's about time. I was wondering if there was something the matter with you," she said.

No, nothing is the matter; but nothing is the same, either. Nothing will ever be the same. The two of us are going to be the three of us. I might call some of those tabloids myself!

Heavenly Father, you created a new being in us, and now you are creating another through us. Thank you for those who care enough to share the joy and for the doctors who helped us. But thank you especially for entrusting us with the care of your creation.

Preparing the Way

◆

I go to prepare a place for you.
John 14:2

Once their emotional and spiritual pulse is quickened with the knowledge that they are going to become parents, people take stock of their surroundings. The scales that were on their eyes in regard to living conditions fall off, just as they did for their internal eyes. Is the apartment or house big enough? It definitely isn't clean enough. Mothers-to-be may check the floors and immediately begin scrubbing them, because of the crawling about to take place. Fathers-to-be may ask if the garage is organized enough, as if the new baby is going to need to get some tiny hands on that crescent wrench in a hurry.

When you've never had a person come to stay in this fashion before, you don't know exactly how to get the place ready.

When the scales fell off our outward eyes, we didn't like what we saw. It was okay for *us* to have a spotty, mostly dead, water-repellent yard, but with a new baby coming we knew we needed to clean it up. The inside of the house hadn't been painted for years. Those ugly blinds would have to go. We wanted to make a good first impression.

I had never believed in reincarnation, so it wasn't as if I thought this baby had been to a lot of houses before and might think poorly of this one. But the knowledge that a baby is coming changes everything. Even though you've never been a parent, you want the baby to think you're an old hand at this, that you are familiar with the latest trends, that you know what good conditions are. In case the baby has a pipeline back to those yet to be born, you don't want word getting out that they should avoid your house.

If the gender of the baby is known, parents can decorate the nursery more specifically. And nursery decoration is a big deal. It needs to communicate to the baby that you didn't just throw something together last night. It needs a theme. Our culture demands nothing less.

But for me it was really not a cultural expectation as much as an indicator of the adequacy question. If I do this nursery right, I can move on to the more complicated matters of being a dad. There's no escaping this feeling.

It is possible to know what the baby's gender will be. But there's no rule that says just because it is possible that it is also necessary. We chose not to know our baby's gender, so we were fairly neutral in getting the room ready. Being a transplanted Minnesotan, I liked the idea of surrounding the baby with hockey players and replicas of the Stanley Cup. But I'm also a news buff, so a "60 Minutes" theme sounded good—I proposed a mobile with stuffed stopwatches hanging over the crib.

We agreed on teddy bears.

And it was in the act of washing the walls of the baby's room, sanding the doors, painting, that my fear of inadequacy began to give way to excitement. Thinking about this person who had never been here, but who really belonged here—a guest, but really a resident, someone we didn't know, but whom we had always known, because we were in on the creation—made me more careful in how I painted and cleaned. It was an incarnation experience I had felt at no Christmas season. This wasn't a guest. This was royalty. But family. It was baffling.

While we worked on the room we discussed names for this new person we had always known yet had never met. In a way, choosing a name for a baby determines many things about him or her. It determines the first impression from others—will he or she be taken seriously, or will others smirk when they are first introduced? In the church where I grew up a family named their girls Bambi and Fawn. We speculated that a third sibling would be named Shamu. Think about the importance of a name. If my daughter ended up writing about toxic waste for the *New York Times* and her byline was "by Thumper Nelson," would anyone take that story seriously?

And how important is it to name the person after a significant family member or Bible character? My dad's name is Elmer Theodore, and my mother-in-law's name is Muriel. But those seemed like names from another era. What about Samson? Delilah? We had seen the name Hannah a lot, and there were a lot of good disciples' names out there, with the exceptions of Judas and Thaddeus.

What would we call this new creature? How would it affect this person's life?

We decided to at least give our boy the middle name Cunningham, after my hero, my grandfather. The name Blake sounded good with Cunningham. I didn't mind that one of my editor friends said it sounded like a name for the Most Valuable Player of the World Series.

A girl's name is easy to get cute with. We had all heard about Crystal Shanda Lear. I had a student named Honey

Bunch. We weren't going to do that to our daughter. I remembered James Dobson telling of how proud he and his wife were when they came up with a name for their daughter—Danae—and how devastated they were when they heard kids at school calling her Decay. The name for our possible daughter eventually came as Marie Kathleen—a combination of the names of my wife's sister and aunt. It fit our criteria of sounding good and having character and meaning.

On a human level, we were doing for our baby what God does for us all the time. We were preparing a place, trying to provide protection for the future. The painting and the discussing of names were things we could do to make the way special for our baby. I'm beginning to understand the depth of God's love for us a little bit better.

Heavenly Father, thank you for all you do to prepare the way for your children. Help us to see your work in making the way better, and give us the power and the vision to do the same for our children.

From Anticipation Back to Faith

By faith our ancestors received approval.

Hebrews 11:2

There is another kind of preparation necessary for bringing a baby into the world. The other preparation is for the mom's body, so the baby can actually get to that newly painted nursery. There is a certain expectation among women that, yes, this birth will be uncomfortable or even excruciating, but there is a simultaneous desire to make the baby's entry with as little trauma as possible.

We attended childbirth classes with eleven other couples. Some of the women looked and acted as if being pregnant was the best thing that ever happened to them. They were radiant. Others did not exude this joy. One woman, in her twenties, said she had had a baby eleven years ago in an army hospital and it was the worst experience of her life.

Some of the women came alone to the classes, even though they were supposed to have a "coach" with them to assist when push really came to shove. I wondered if the women without coaches ever felt more alone in their lives. I wondered how they would manage after the baby was born.

The coaches, mostly husbands, mothers, or roommates, were in constant motion. They were always rubbing something on the expectant women—shoulders, arms, elbows, knees, scalps, lower backs, upper backs, ankles, necks—not in a slow, relaxing fashion, but in a staccato, almost compulsive way.

It was as if they were saying, "Isn't this great and won't the birth experience be a blast and I'm sorry you're the one who has to go through it. I wish it could be me instead, but it wasn't me who bit the apple first in Eden, and I guess I can't really identify with the pain you're going to experience, so I guess I'll just rub a hole right through the sleeve of your sweater while I sit here and thank God Almighty that I get to dodge the bullet on this one."

Likewise the mothers-to-be had expressions on their faces that seemed to say, "This is so romantic—I'm so glad we're doing this together, and while you're rubbing my arm trying to relax me don't forget it was your idea to have children. You know I could have waited a couple more years until my career got going and your family has a history of having large-headed babies so you know it won't fit coming out and they'll have to cut me or drug me. Either way I won't be able to stand it or feel it because I'll be so busy trying to decide whether I'll survive it. And if you say 'Relax, honey' even once while I'm grabbing my knees and screaming for the doctor to call 911 I personally will see to it that you will never father a child again."

It's all part of having a baby together.

But behind the glimmer of anticipation for this miracle is anxiety. "Will my labor be as bad as my sister's or mother's? Will the baby be healthy? How can I find out now? Will the baby be happy we brought her here? Will she want to keep us as her parents? Will she cry all the time so we won't get any sleep and make us all extremely irritable for the next few years? Will I be a good parent? Will the baby be as bright as my boss's kids? Will the baby love me as much as I already love him or her? Is that possible?"

I started to think of the baby growing up. Is there some way I can help her avoid the pain that goes with being a child? The disappointments, the rejections? At least the *serious* pain and rejection? Can I lay that groundwork now so that my child will know mostly joy? What can I do to make my child's stay on this planet a happy one?

My smile of anticipation was transformed into a frown, and I rubbed my wife's back more vigorously.

In our small group, one couple lost their baby and another delivered a healthy one several weeks early. It was horrible for one and wonderful for the other. I couldn't help but wonder what we might experience.

By the end of six weeks the mother-to-be and the coach are well-versed in breathing techniques, visualizing what the baby is doing with each contraction, and the options regarding rooms. One could request a private room or go in a larger ward and risk getting stuck with three women screaming terrible things at their husbands.

Our class disbanded with the promise that we would regroup once we had all delivered. It was a festive parting, for we had all shared a small part of something miraculous with one another.

And yet . . . would we all be this cheery a month or two from now? The instructor told me privately that statistics showed some of our group would be divorced within a year of the baby's birth. There are so many hidden traumas; couples aren't ready for the pressure, she said.

I don't think of myself as a worst-case scenario person, but I felt myself becoming one. Is worry a faith issue? Of course it is. But now, with the stakes this high—healthy, happy baby, solid marriage, adequate parent—it's not so easy to just "turn them over" to God.

As I pondered this I realized I was trying to do something impossible—I was trying to turn the birth over to God, the baby's health over to God, the child's happiness over to God, my marriage over to God. The piecemeal approach never works, though. I needed to turn *myself* over to God.

Father, I want to know it is going to be okay. But I can't know that. So please show me that, no matter what happens, I am your child and I can rest in you.

Being Known Completely

◆

My [body] was not hidden from you. . . .
Such knowledge is too wonderful for me.
Psalm 139:15, 6

With the availability of advanced technology come choices that parents of previous generations never had to make. Mentioned earlier was the option of knowing the baby's gender. Another possibility is knowing whether the baby is healthy. If not, that knowledge presents parents with additional choices. The very things that are presumed to simplify our lives can instead complicate them.

We chose to have an ultrasound, a test in which the baby is bombarded with sound waves and the parents can watch the outline of the baby on a television screen. We were a little nervous, because it was during an ultrasound test that friends of ours discovered their baby had died. I wanted to see this little person, but I didn't want to find out about a problem.

When we finally saw the baby on the screen, this little swimmer looked ready for the Olympics! The shadow pushed off one side of my wife's insides, got to the other, and pushed off from there. Okay, so the baby was moving so much to escape the sound waves, but at least we knew this person was there and could tread water.

The doctor pointed out the spine, the skull, and some other bones, but said the gender was still unknown. At that stage of development the baby looked perfect.

Then we listened to all of this activity. The heartbeat was strong and at a normal rate, even though it sounded as if someone had taken the top off a washing machine. We listened in on this mysterious traveler. We saw. We heard. We knew the baby was really there. We could see what was going on now when before all we could do was feel the motion from the outside.

For us the ultrasound was verification that no, this wasn't just wishful thinking on our part; there was a real, live baby in there, and one of these days he or she was going to come out to meet us. No one could say *for sure* that an apparently normal baby was in there until the ultrasound and the assurance from the doctor. We felt a lot of relief. Our faith got a healthy dose of substance with that doctor's visit.

At a surface level we felt that we began to know the baby. We saw, listened, and could identify this new presence. But we only knew the baby as far as today. We didn't know what our baby would be like, how this person would spend life on the planet. It is even more unfathomable, then, to ponder these thoughts from Psalm 139:

> *You hem me in, behind and before,*
> *and lay your hand upon me. . . .*
> *For it was you who formed my inward parts;*
> *you knit me together in my mother's womb*
> *(Psalm 139:5, 13).*

What we saw was an outline of our baby. Verse 14 of this psalm says God knows us "through and through," at a level beyond ultrasound or any other human understanding. I don't even know *myself* through and through, yet God knows our baby this way and is keeping a close guard before and behind. That is something I can rest in.

About a month before the baby was due I was preparing to leave for a week of important business. Well, okay, it was for a week of skiing in Utah. But it was important skiing. And because the pregnancy had been going well, we agreed it would be all right for me to go.

While I was packing, my wife commented that she hadn't felt the baby move much that day. I wasn't worried but commented that she is normally very still on weekday mornings at work, when the baby's movements would be more noticeable. And because this was Saturday and we were working around the house, no activity sensation was explainable, I said.

About two hours later I walked into the bedroom and saw my wife on the bed, sobbing, silent, nearly hysterical. "I can't get him to move at all," she said.

She had taken drinks of fruit juice, soda, anything she could to get him stirring, but it hadn't worked. Neither of us mentioned the couple in our childbirth class who had lost their baby, but we each knew what the other was thinking. I put my hands on her stomach and felt for myself. She was right, of course. I spoke loudly to her stomach, sang, jostled her back and forth, and got only a slight sense of motion. The baby moved a bit more as the day went on.

The Utah trip didn't seem very important suddenly, yet we had both heard about in–utero growth spurts when the baby sleeps a lot, and about how some days the baby just wants to take it easy for a while. To cancel the trip seemed excessive at the time, as long as he was moving some.

I told a colleague about it on the airplane that night, tears running down my face, and his reply was, "This is only the first scare of many." He has a sixteen-year-old daughter and a nine-year-old son. The daughter is recovering from a serious car accident in which she was the driver. The son nearly drowned as a baby in their swimming pool.

I called when I got to Utah and my wife said the baby had moved much more during the evening. It occurred to me that night that our baby might not turn out all right after all. But God knew this baby through and through, and me through and through, and my wife through and through. That much I knew, and it was worth hanging on to.

I pray with the psalmist today, O God, that you search me and know my thoughts today, test me and understand my misgivings. Watch in case I follow any path that grieves you, and guide me in your ways. You created me. You know me. I am yours.

Addressing the 'What If?'

◆

Therefore, let those suffering in accordance with God's will entrust themselves to a faithful Creator, while continuing to do good.

1 Peter 4:19

It is probably every parent-to-be's unspoken fear that there will be something wrong with his or her baby. The odds are tremendous that something will *not* be wrong, and that even if there is something wrong, the technology of today may make things better. There's still that chance, though, and we all wonder if we will be the statistic that we are trying to avoid.

I got a call from an old college roommate who was in town for a conference—we hadn't seen each other for twelve years. He told me that he had four children and that I had a lot of catching up to do if my family were to compete with his.

We got to talking about his twin brother, who had died in a plane crash while we were in college. I asked him how fresh the memory of Bob was.

"It's very fresh, but probably not for the reasons you might think," he said. He explained that, to honor the memory of his brother, he and his wife had named their son after Bob. After their boy was born, though, they realized he had Down syndrome.

"We named him to preserve Bob's memory, but he's retarded," my friend said. "Pretty ironic."

It sounded like a cruel joke.

We've had the sonogram for our baby and we saw two arms and two legs and a spine. In all probability our baby did not have Down syndrome, the doctor said (we asked specifically). But that was the message my former roommate had gotten, too. Even if we knew now that our baby was going to be retarded, would that change anything? I don't think so.

I know of cases where a Down syndrome baby resulted in the family's breaking up. The pressure, the disappointment, the extra work was just too much of a strain. Yet I also know of a situation in which the presence of a helplessly handicapped boy was a source of tremendous strength to the family. The story, in the book *The Power of the Powerless*, by Christopher De Vinck, tells how a doctor told the family that the baby was a vegetable and should probably be institutionalized for the few months he would live. The mother refused to go home from the hospital without him. "He is our son," she said.

The family set up a room for the baby. They spoon-fed him through life, changed his diapers, and rolled him over to pound his back so he could breathe. He lived for more than thirty years. The person who wrote the book is the "vegetable's" brother. He said that his bedridden, helpless, dependent brother was the most loving, inspirational, and powerful person he knew. He illustrates with an anecdote. When the writer was young, he brought a girl over to the house to meet his family. The introduction included the brother upstairs. The girlfriend shivered at the sight and couldn't walk into the room. Sometime later, he brought another girl to the house and introduced her. Then he began to feed his brother. This girl asked, "Can I feed him?" The writer asked the reader, "Guess which girl I married?"

The book gave me new insight into what was possible with a child with problems. But was I equipped to put my life on hold while we sought the right care? Was one of us equipped to drop out of life so that we could provide the care ourselves? Perhaps I had been operating on the assumption that I had a right to a healthy child.

At no point in the book did the author say his family asked "Why us?" The truer question for my family, I suppose, would be "Why *not* us?" My cousins asked this question when their daughter was struck by a car and put into a long-term coma. They said, "Who is better equipped to deal with tragedy than those whose faith is in God and not in their circumstances?" I wondered if I would be that mature, that alert to the peace and comfort of God's hand.

I confess that I struggle with 1 Peter 3:14-15 when I consider the possibility that we will have a less-than-perfectly developed child: "But even if you do suffer for doing what is right, you are blessed. Do not fear what they fear, and do not be intimidated, but in your hearts sanctify Christ as Lord."

Would I have any hope if my baby were like my roommate's? This was a spiritual valley for me. I know people who have tried to make deals with God, and others who have tried to arrange his promises in such a way that supposedly God had no choice but to give them what they wanted. "Since God can't lie, just make sure you ask in such a way that he has to answer your request," one person told me. "Then it's a slam dunk."

Somehow, likening God's action to a basketball move struck me as an unattractive view of God. As I read the Bible I see God as someone not to be figured out, but to be worshiped. How can I worship God when I am trying to manipulate him?

There is something I can do, 1 Peter 4:19 says. I can commit myself to God. And there is something God will do, it says.

He will not fail me. How do I prepare myself for being the father of a sick baby? Commit myself to God. How do I prepare myself for being the father of a healthy baby? Commit myself to God. And what will God do? He will not fail me.

This is what empowers my old college roommate and his family. His son has taught them a lot, he told me, about love without conditions. "Robby loves purely," my roommate said, "and he draws a pure love response out of us." Sounds a lot like the love of God, doesn't it? The word for today is that the love of God is the only guarantee. My roommate says it is enough.

Heavenly Father, it seems as if I have something new to be afraid of every day. I'm afraid of having a sick baby and of not being able to see you in it. Fill my fear with hope, my weakness with love. Show me that you are enough.

The Permanence of Parenthood

He put a new song in my mouth.
Psalm 40:3

What does it mean to become a parent? I mean besides the obvious stuff like changing diapers, heating bottles, writing thank-you notes, picking up clumps of dog hair in the corners, arranging for photo sessions, giving rides to swimming lessons, working in the church nursery, helping out with the Little League team, going to parent-teacher meetings, arguing with the high school principal, having a graduation open house, clearing out a room after college, and calling friends to see if they'll hire your son or daughter?

What does it mean, deep down inside the mom and dad?

My wife and I would address this at the oddest times—working in the yard, making the bed, eating dinner, driving in the car. "What will we do the first time he or she has to stay after school because of a discipline problem?" My wife likes to think ahead. I'm wondering how I'm going to get my work done on little sleep the first few weeks, and she has him misbehaving in school, possibly ten years from now.

But we both were after a similar concept: What does it mean to become a *good* parent? What does it take? When does love need common sense? Where does common sense come from if you've never had kids before? When does discipline need to give way to latitude? When does everything else in the world need to stop in order to give attention to the son or daughter? When does everything need to continue? Can you love a child too much? Is it all just a giant gamble? Where are the rules? How do you know when you've broken them? It seemed that parenting was a lot like journalism—there is no one way to do it, but when you do it badly you look really stupid and the whole world knows it.

And when should God be part of the equation? Of course the answer is "always," but when is the child introduced to the nature of God? What if the parents are a little fuzzy on the nature of God themselves? If there is confusion about God in the parents' lives, is there any hope for the children?

We knew there was a lot that we could not learn about parenting until we were in the middle of it, but it seemed there were a lot of smart people out there who could help prepare us for some of it.

In a matter of months my wife had become an expert in fetal development and childrearing. I never saw her study this hard in college or graduate school. She had an insatiable desire to know *exactly* what the baby looked like at each week of pregnancy. She would bring a book to bed and read to me: "The heart is now inside the body," or "The stomach is completely formed; hair is beginning to come in," or "The baby has fingernails now." And with each new development came an increased desire to know more about what to do when the baby arrived.

I guess because it wasn't happening inside my body I didn't have the same intensity for knowing what the daily or weekly physiological changes were. I was more concerned about being ready for parenthood. I read several books by fathers, read other books about parenting written by psychologists—some Christian and some not—and talked a great deal with other fathers. One man told me that he still lives in fear of being a total failure as a father (his kids are thirteen and six) and wants this epitaph on his tombstone: He didn't mess up.

I encounter college students every day who have tremendous stories of family life. They are well-adjusted largely because of the quality of parenting they received. Conversely, I see potentially high achievers who do nothing with themselves because their self-esteem has been trampled so low by inadequate parents.

Which will I be?

It was evident to us that changes were taking place in our home before the arrival of this baby. Besides the cleaner rug and yard, I mean. Value changes were occurring—how we spent our time, how we spent our money, what we thought about, what kind of influence we wanted to be, what we believed about God. These things weren't as crucial to us before we knew we were becoming parents.

The knowledge of what was to come had already changed us. Once a person becomes a parent (and I believed we already were at this point), the act can't be undone. You can't *un*father someone. You can divorce a spouse. You can change political parties. You can quit a job in Los Angeles and move to Alaska to live in the wild. You can be *un*faithful and *un*-American. But even if the baby dies, it won't make you an *un*parent. That's a done deal forever.

These thoughts drove me to a pad of paper to write about anticipation of the baby's arrival. We still didn't know the gender, so for simplicity's sake I presumed one.

In one earth-arresting moment
you
changed, vaulting from
anticipated guest
(we had your room ready—painted walls, stuffed animals)
to beautiful son
bigger than life.

With a double-edged beginning
you
too, created
mother and father who
had their dreams ready—new capacities, intense
feelings
and now marvel at
the world again.

This baby was a new creature. So were his mom and dad.

Heavenly Father, thank you for the gift of life—for new life. Thank you for the new life we have in you. Thank you for the new life of our baby. Thank you for the new life of becoming a parent.

Learning to Walk Humbly

◆

Humble yourselves therefore
under the mighty hand of God,
so that he may exalt you in due time.
1 Peter 5:6

Nothing can adequately prepare parents for witnessing the birth of their shared creation. Not only is it beyond comprehension, but human language fails miserably when one tries to describe the event. We've all heard the stories, and they all have a certain sameness to them. Frankly, other people's birth stories aren't that interesting. Until a person *experiences* this . . . this . . . explosion of intensity and wonder, the descriptions might as well be in a foreign language.

As a member of an ambulance crew and as an orderly for both emergency and operating rooms, I had seen lots of births. Some in hallways, some in speeding vans, some scheduled weeks in advance, some without warning. All were amazing. But as an orderly I was more impressed with the doctors or paramedics than I was with God or with how life perpetuates itself.

Childbirth classes try to prepare couples for the event by showing videos of people giving birth. I thought they looked a lot like the movies that are shown in drivers' training classes. The people who brought us *Blood on the Highway* and *The Last*

Drive Home undoubtedly were in on these. One movie showed fourteen families giving birth, one right after the other. The women bossed their husbands around and snapped at them when the husbands tried to suggest ways to help. The most brutal words were for those who tried to tell their wives to relax. I remember looking around at the other husbands in my class, and we all nodded to each other as we filed that one away in permanent storage.

At the end of the movie all of the women were holding their babies, beaming, crying, talking about what a wonderful experience it was, and how much they loved their husbands. None of the coaches in my class believed them. We were terrified.

I walked the hallways of an entire hospital floor on our big day and tried to keep up with my wife's strides, holding her IV bottle aloft with one hand like the Olympic torch and rubbing her lower back with the other. As is her pattern in the rest of her life, she wanted to be moving during the contractions. If I fell behind or didn't rub hard enough it was curtly brought to my attention.

When the doctor arrived he calmly told my wife, "So let's have the baby." For some babies, that's all the encouragement they need. They breeze out and in moments are potty-trained. For others—ours, for instance—encouragement was not enough. My wife pushed hard for more than an hour. It was excruciating for her. She was nearly unconscious with fatigue when our little boy finally appeared. But oh, what an appearance!

He squawked a couple of times, but mostly just moved his head around as if to see who was there. He began to cry and the doctor handed him to me. I wept openly as Blake allowed me to hold him close and welcome him to the outside world. My first instinct was to introduce myself to him and tell him that he was in a safe place, that we would take care of him, that he could trust us. I made promises to him—that I would always love him, that I would always protect him, that I would always be there for him. I promised him the moon.

I put him on my wife's stomach, but after more than twenty hours of intense pain, her throbbing body was too unsteady. It was time for all of us to rest, and to never be the same again.

After he was cleaned and weighed and we got into our room for the night, I went outside. It was about 1:30 A.M. The street was still and dark, unmoved by the earthshaking event that had just taken place.

A low rumble began shaking the area and I watched from the front sidewalk as a helicopter appeared over the trees and landed on the hospital roof. People rushed around the rooftop as if someone's life depended on them.

It dawned on me then how much I had taken for granted that Blake was healthy. My fear of his having some severe problem disappeared without a trace when he appeared. And here I was watching someone being flown to an emergency room because something had gone terribly wrong, something that could have an abrupt and tragic ending, just minutes after watching something go very right, something with a mostly peaceful, very happy outcome—just as I expected.

I wondered what I would be thinking had something gone wrong in the delivery room—an errant move by the doctor, a badly developed body, a previously undetected disease—what then? Would I be saying "Why us?" Would I be bitter? Angry at God? Or would I ask, like my dear cousin, "Why *not* us? Who is better equipped to deal with pain than those who have experienced the love of God?"

When the helicopter finally departed, perhaps for another tragedy, I was awestruck by what a gamble it all is. We think we have a right to health, but we all know righteous, godly people who have had imperfect children and whose lives have been substantially altered because of it. Walking back into the hospital, taking the elevator to see my wife and perfect child, I was humbled by what God had given us that night.

In the room, a nurse was helping Blake and my wife learn about breast feeding. He was getting it. My last thought of the night as I stretched out on the portable bed was, "He's finally here and he's catching on." I hoped I caught on to fatherhood as quickly.

> *Lord, what a wonder you are! What a wonderful gift you have given us. You have humbled me with your love and perfect creation. Make me a good father. Make me like you.*

How Different Life Is Together

◆

I pray that you may have the power to comprehend . . . what is the breadth and length and height and depth, and to know the love of Christ.
Ephesians 3:18

It is difficult to remember what life was like B.C.—Before Children—even when the baby is just a few weeks old. What, exactly, was an uninterrupted night of sleep? It's history. What was it like to just pick up at the last minute and go to the mountains for the weekend? I've forgotten. Now it takes an act of Congress to get all the paraphernalia in the car, have materials for every type of emergency, and anticipate all of the things that will keep trips to the store to a minimum—and that is just to go on a picnic at a nearby park.

New parents feel guilty for thinking these things because they fear it sounds as if they are longing for those days of being without children. That isn't what they want at all. But the amazing gift of children is a very complicating one that takes more time and energy than anyone without children can imagine. In some respects it is similar to embarking on a journey with the Lord. People sometimes think that, when they accept Christ, everything falls into place and life becomes one happy moment after another.

Not so. Not with Christ, and not with children. But life is clearly better with Christ, not simpler; and for my family, life is clearly better, not simpler, with a baby in the house. I wonder if God ever considers what life was like before there were people. No doubt things were simpler.

Remember what a precious thing a Saturday was? Mine used to be (as I recall with my ever-diminishing memory) along the line of: awaken early, but not because I had to; grind some coffee; read the newspaper from beginning to end, and maybe even read some previous days' editions if I had missed them; walk around the house to take inventory of what needed to be done that day; slowly start some of those tasks, taking ample time to rest and reflect; sit in the sun at the beach or in the yard; and watch whatever teams were competing in whatever sports on television. Now *that's* a Saturday.

One Saturday during Blake's first month I thought I got up early enough to sneak in some coffee and the newspaper before he woke up. I even ground the coffee the night before in anticipation of the next morning's privacy. Nice try. His crying brought me running from the kitchen just as I was turning on the coffeepot. I wanted to get him before he woke my wife. It was Saturday for her, too. I tried reading the paper with him in my lap, but it was a wrestling match. Getting through it was a hollow victory.

One of the results of having a baby in the house is that the parents, by necessity, become extremely productive in a very short amount of time. On that same Saturday, during Blake's two-hour nap, I washed the car, mowed the lawn, climbed a tree to prune the branches, bundled up the branches, and did general cleanup in the garage. On a before-Blake Saturday this would have taken me all weekend.

Evenings are the same way. Some people like to read in the evening. Some like to watch television. Once they have children they wonder what those days felt like.

On the one hand it is hard not to envy those with more free time. In one of my more insensitive moments I remember asking some friends if they ever felt cheated because they never had children. They are about fifteen years older than my wife and me, and it was a safe bet that they weren't going to expand their family. We have traveled across Europe and the South Pacific with them, but they won't curtail their travel because we can't go now. They'll just go without us.

"Cheated? No, not cheated," was the man's reply. "But I'll always be curious about what a child would have been like, what kind of dad I would have been, how life would be different with that new dimension. We'll never know life the way you know it," he said.

Having a productive Saturday didn't mean quite as much to me after that conversation.

Another dad told me how surprised he was at the potentially violent feelings he had when it came to protecting his son. Normally a quiet, shy guy, he told about seeing a kid in his neighborhood drive around the corner too fast. The car came close to hitting the curb near the sidewalk where my friend was pushing his new baby in the stroller.

"I yelled to my wife to watch the baby and I took off running after the car," he said. The driver didn't see the enraged dad, so he pulled into the driveway of his nearby house and got out. The dad shoved him back into the car and told him how badly he would be beaten if the dad ever saw him drive like that again when kids were around.

"I realized then that I had the capacity to kill someone to protect my child," he said.

But it's not just primal rage that is uncovered with children. There is a primal love as well.

When Blake was about two weeks old Marcia went out for an evening. I must have convinced her of my competence, because she only called the house once. Blake and I had a ball. We listened to Garrison Keillor's "Prairie Home Companion" on the radio, I watched some basketball while Blake tore up an entire roll of toilet paper, and we snoozed.

I'm not sure there is any other feeling comparable to lying on your back, baby on chest, with his feet and hands curled up between your bodies, and both of you sleeping soundly. It's a position of poetry. Partial creator with his creation. Both deeply in love with the other. And though I may think about what life was like before him, I don't long for it.

Father, this new life is a gift from you. Thank you for the reminders our babies give us of how deep and wide and unfathomable your love is for us. We understand it a little better because of the deep love we have for our children.

When Joy Is Shared

◆

I came that they may have life,
and have it abundantly.
John 10:10

Fathers like taking their babies with them wherever they go. They take them hiking, they take them across the stage at college graduation, they take them to company picnics, to ball games, and on errands. I liked to take Blake around the house with me, draped lengthwise on my forearm. There's something energizing about having the baby with you at all times, in part so you won't miss some new act or sound. It is part of the parents' new definition of joy: seeing your baby do something new. It is an amendment to Jesus' desire for us to enjoy the abundant life.

I would have missed the first time Blake bit and swallowed part of my Nerf indoor croquet set had I not been carrying him with me from room to room. The second and third times weren't nearly as joyful or abundant.

My wife believes I took that togetherness sentiment too far when he was five months old.

I'm no astrologer, but when Halley's comet appeared in the sky and the Minnesota Twins appeared in the World Series the same year, I knew that something otherworldy was going on and that I needed to be in on it with my son.

I remember the excitement throughout Minnesota when the former Washington Senators moved to Minneapolis. I remember having school cancelled when the Twins went to the Series against Sandy Koufax and Don Drysdale of the Los Angeles Dodgers. There was no World Series championship that year, but then, there was no comet, either. The comet was a sign, much like Noah's rainbow, I told Marcia. Everything would go the Twins' way and it was my right—nay, my duty as a former Minnesotan—to go the opening game in Minneapolis. And to take Blake with me, of course.

What happened next would turn a weaker person into a New Ager, for sure. My dad got two tickets for the first game and said he would let me have one. Well, what he really said was, "If you're crazy enough to come, you can have a ticket, but you have to bring the baby so we can see him."

Then, the day before the game, one of the editors I work for called to tell me I had won a local journalism award for a series of investigative stories I had written for his newspaper. The cash award covered the cost of a ticket to Minneapolis and back.

Even Marcia couldn't argue with how all of this was looking. Her concern, naturally, was whether Blake would be okay. But since I had been taking care of him by myself a few days a week already, she knew I could handle it. "I don't want him to think that I'm not around anymore," she said. She needed him to need her, which he does, of course. But we'd only be gone two days, I countered. And I brought up Halley's comet again.

"In 75 years the comet will return. That's how long it will be before the Twins are in the World Series again," I prophesied. (If you follow baseball you are aware of my miscalculation: the Twins repeated as world champions four years later. But I still have my Homer Hanky, so who cares?)

Blake and I told a very nervous mom and wife good-bye as we boarded the plane at 7 A.M. the next day. I felt confident that he would be okay and that I would know how to keep him happy. Most of the passengers seemed genuinely friendly toward this dad and his baby. They were even helpful. But not as helpful as the flight attendants. I must have looked incompetent, because soon after we were airborne they took him all over the plane and played with him. I caught up on some sleep.

This apparent reverse sexism was the opposite treatment my wife got when she had flown with him two months previously. She was carrying a new baby, an overstuffed diaper bag, and a car seat, and was treated badly. A dad appears with a baby, though, and it is presumed he needs help. Interesting.

I didn't improve my quest for competency when I was trying to get Blake to quiet down for a nap. I was standing at the front of this full plane, in the aisle, jostling him on my shoulder and humming softly to him. Hundreds of people behind me smiled at the sight. The flight attendants came down the same narrow path with their food trays, so I stepped up out of their way and mashed Blake's nearly asleep face into the luggage rack.

Have you ever heard 200 people gasp in unison? I'm surprised it didn't slow the plane down to have that much air taken out of the cabin at once. Soon after that more help arrived.

We changed planes twice before we arrived in Minneapolis that afternoon. Diaper changes took place in the cramped bathroom, with Blake's torso on the narrow counter and his legs in the sink. He was fascinated with the bright red emergency call button, so it was a trick to keep his hands away from that and clean his lower body.

But we made it, my folks were thrilled, the Twins won, and the next day we were back on the plane. Once again it was confirmed that taking the trip was the right thing: the plane had the same flight crew as the day before. I barely saw my son on the way home.

When we got home Blake clearly recognized Marcia and cooed and pounded his arms on her back as she held him. They had each other in a locked grip that lasted most of the evening. At the house he giggled and rolled around on the floor as if everything Marcia said was hysterically funny. It was clear that the three of us belonged together, not apart.

Still, it was a historic weekend and I'd do it again in a minute. To share the experience with a baby whose nature it is to trust you, and with a wife who chooses to trust you, was a new kind of joy.

> *Father, sometimes our joy takes us to the extreme. Thank you for this new capacity to enjoy life. Thank you for a family that likes to share in unconventional ways of having fun. Thank you for being a God who enjoys the lives of his creation.*

The Need for Stability

◆

Make me to know your ways, O L*ORD;*
teach me your paths.
Psalm 25:4

There was a popular song about three decades ago that had these lyrics: "What the world needs now is love, sweet love. It's the only thing that there's just too little of." Most high school small groups sang arrangements of it, and it was even rerecorded during turbulent times in the United States as an effort to get the nation calmed down again. We all believed that those lyrics were true, although the song didn't tell how more love could be attained.

Now that I am sensitive to matters of fatherhood, I don't believe those lyrics are true anymore. I've talked with too many fathers, and with too many sons and daughters about their fathers. What the world needs now are stable, mentally healthy moms and dads who love God and take their roles as parents seriously. *That's* what there's just too little of.

I read in several books that how Marcia and I interact with Blake before he is five will determine how he will interact with the rest of the world. After he starts school we are no longer his primary influence; we become one of many. I also know dozens of people who have difficulty managing in this world because of the unstable treatment they got at home.

A college friend who had spent the last fifteen years hating his parents was in a near-fatal accident and spent three months recovering at his parents' house. He had been in therapy for years trying to cope with the anger he felt toward his parents, particularly his father. The anger affected his job, his relationships, his run-ins with the law. After the accident he was an invalid with childlike needs, and his parents became caretakers again.

After he had largely recovered he was at my house and, while showing off my new son, I jokingly said I didn't know whether I wanted Blake to win a Pulitzer prize or the Stanley Cup hockey championship. Maybe he'd be the first to win both, I said. My friend wasn't amused.

"Don't lay that on him or you'll be sorry," he said.

"I was only kidding."

"You were only partly kidding."

He was right, of course.

A great renewal occurred during my friend's stay with his parents. With the help of counseling, they found that much of the problem was in the twisted way the parents told him how much they loved him. As a boy, when my friend didn't live up to his parents' expectations, his dad beat him. Now, fifteen years later, they are all getting a second chance.

When I was in high school I worked part-time as an orderly in a county general hospital's emergency room. A little girl was brought in one night with multiple bruises and vaginal injuries inflicted by her father. She lay on the examining table, eyes wide open, in shock.

"I'd like to get my hands on that father," I proclaimed to the doctor.

"Really? What would you do?"

"He deserves to die for something like this," I said. Teenagers have a wonderful sense of justice.

"I suspect you'll feel differently when you have your own children," the doctor said. "There isn't a human on this planet, including yourself, who isn't capable of some form of abuse to one of his own children under extreme circumstances."

Uncontrolled emotions seem to be the root of people growing up to be unstable. And it's not as easy as saying if parents only knew Jesus, the problem would disappear. Marcia and I were in the home of some Christian friends for dinner several years ago, and their little boy spilled his milk after repeated warnings from the dad to be careful. As fast as lightning the dad swept the boy out of his chair and beat him severely on the dining room floor.

I can't imagine that I'm capable of that kind of behavior, but, given some awful circumstances, maybe I could lose control too. Maybe with little sleep over several months, no extra help from a spouse, trouble at work, maybe being out of work, trouble between the husband and wife—maybe I could be driven to being that out of control.

I want to be the kind of father who will make Blake feel comfortable enough with himself and his surroundings that he won't have to sit in a counselor's office and bare his soul because he didn't get the care and attention he needed at home.

Erma Bombeck says that guilt is the gift that keeps on giving. I'm feeling as if the gift has been deposited in my house in a big way.

Is Blake's mental health really up to Marcia and me? In large part, yes. How does that affect the time I spend at home, and how much time I am away from home? Is Blake my priority or is my work? What about my relationship with Marcia? Can they all be priorities?

In *The Celebration of Discipline*, Richard Foster's classic treatment of the spiritual disciplines, he tells of going into his children's rooms after they were asleep and praying for them. He would lay his hands on them and pray that God would fill them with his being and protect them, that they would love God. That sounds like a positive step toward mental health.

As with anything involving parenting, there is more risk than certainty. I can't be certain that Blake will be a healthy, stable, well-adjusted man who will love God. But if *I* strive for those things for myself, and Marcia strives for herself, and we live out a healthy life in front of our son, I believe the risk diminishes.

Heavenly Father, as parents we are terrified of bringing up unstable people in an already unstable world. Give us the stability of your ways, your truths. Give us the power to leave ourselves and our children in your perfect hands.

Letters to Fathers

◆

Is there anyone among you who,
if your child asks for bread,
will give a stone?
Matthew 7:9

Some of the greatest advice on being a dad comes from kids. In 1989 the *Minneapolis Star Tribune* newspaper asked young people to write in with comments on their fathers. "It's one of the most profound influences on our lives, coloring our perceptions and shaping our destinies," said the reporter in the March 7 introduction. "Yet none of us has any choice in the matter. Who fathers us is determined by chance, fate, maybe divine decision—and we are born blessed or burdened."

The newspaper asked what advice young people would like to give to their own fathers specifically and to fathers generally. It was easy to choose which fathers you wanted to be like and which ones you wanted to avoid.

Some children wrote about dads who helped them take care of their hamsters, who assisted with homework, who stayed calm during crises, who attended recitals and games, who took care of them when they were sick, and who cooked their favorite meals when they felt lousy.

"When I was a little girl my dad would get me up in the morning, make breakfast for me and do my hair because my mom had to go to work before I was ever awake," wrote a thirteen-year-old. "I will never forget that."

An eleven-year-old boy didn't paint as glowing a picture of his dad. "I hate those stupid threats I get! 'Shape up or your mother will have to take you off the wall with a spatula.' Ugh."

A seven-year-old girl wrote: "Dear Dad, don't fight with Mom. It hurts my ears."

The most common advice was that dads should spend more time at home, and should listen more and yell less. Many wrote that their fathers place work, watching TV, playing video games, drinking and hanging out with their buddies over spending time with their children. "Talking doesn't take that much energy and a hug isn't very tiring either," wrote a fifteen-year-old. Another teenager wrote, "I understand that he needs time alone or away from home, especially with my parents' marital problems; however, I can't see this as an excuse for running away from my sister and me. We are growing up, and once we are grown, we can never go back. Perhaps my dad will realize too late that he missed us."

Is this preaching to you the way it is to me?

Response after response said "Listen." "Listen." "Listen." "Spend time with us." "Listen." "Don't be away so much." "Listen." "Be nice to mom." "Listen." "Don't yell so much." "Listen."

A ten-year-old paid the highest tribute of all, even though she was sadly mistaken in her last point: "I love my dad and wish he could live forever and ever. I think every kid in America thinks the same of their dad."

No, every kid does not feel the same way about his or her dad. Is it too early to be wondering what Blake will write about his dad?

My dad came to visit shortly after Blake was born and we sat at a table together, addressing birth announcements and reminiscing. He and I have always had a good relationship. I don't recall his ever hitting me. He got exasperated plenty of times, and that was usually enough to get me moving. He and my mom *always* had time for my brothers and me. I don't ever recall hearing the words "Not right now" spoken in our house. I know that he made sacrifices in his education and his jobs so he wouldn't have to be away too much and so he wouldn't have to bring home a lot of stress from work. His family came first, and he paid a price professionally for that philosophy.

That day I asked my dad if he ever got tired of my faking everything under the sun to get out of doing the lawn. Did he remember all the times I made him late for work because he had to drop me off at school when I wasted too much time in the morning? Did it bother him that I could will myself to throw up at the dinner table whenever I was told I had to eat Brussels sprouts? What did he *really* think when I crashed mom's car into his car? How about when I got kicked out of college? Twice?

What if Blake turns out like me, and I don't handle it as gracefully? Did he ever get so bothered by me that he wished I hadn't been born?

Even though my questions were serious, my dad couldn't stop laughing. He corrected some of the details of the stories we relived, but he never attempted to answer my questions. All he could do was laugh. I think he saw justice looming on the horizon.

Time will tell if I become a yeller, an unreasonable person who feels so threatened in other areas of his life that he takes it out on his family, a dad who ranks golf above time with his kids. But it seems to me I can make some choices now that will minimize those undesirable traits.

I can listen to the cries of my baby now and take them seriously—and do the same ten and fifteen years from now. I can love my wife in front of Blake now and later so he will see that we value each other. I can reserve time in my schedule now and later so we can experience life together. I can choose to be attentive to God's Word and his instruction as I pray for myself and my family.

I don't want to have to read advice from my son in the newspaper.

Father, fill the choices that we make today with your presence so they will reflect you throughout our lives. Help our children to know you because they have known us. Help us to give them bread instead of stones.

Finding the Body of Christ at Home

◆

Each of you . . . should love his wife as himself.
Ephesians 5:33

As a nonfemale, I find it difficult sometimes to know what my wife *really* values in life. From what I can gather through discussions and reading, some women place a great deal of importance on the first kiss, the first date, the wedding day, being carried across the threshhold, etc. If all of those are important, then it is an easy leap to assuming that the first Mother's Day would be one of those landmark events for my wife. No one has ever said that to me, but it makes sense, doesn't it?

It makes so much sense that I heap even more guilt on myself for forgetting the day in my own house. Self-contempt reached a new level when I discovered my error.

There were plenty of indicators that the day should be different from all other Sundays. We went to church where it was mentioned, went to an organ concert at an outdoor pavilion in a park downtown where the organist played something like "M is for the million times you fed me." I had even sent a Mother's Day card to my own mom, telling her the day had new meaning for me, and that I had new appreciation for her because of the gift of new life in our house. So how did I forget my own wife, mother of our firstborn?

I can only explain it this way. It still felt as if we were babysitting someone else's child. Blake, at five weeks, didn't feel like *our* baby yet, so it wasn't natural to think of Mother's Day as being *Blake's* mother's day.

I considered finding a florist at the last minute to cover my failure, but my wife has an uncanny ability of seeing through lame efforts like that. So I came clean with her and confessed how blind, stupid, and humiliated I felt. She convinced me that she understood, sort of.

This reminded me of advice I got from a guy who has been married more than twenty-five years and whose kids are making a wonderful contribution to society. He said that the greatest parenting trait he knew of was for husbands to love their wives. When kids (even babies) see mom and dad discussing, hugging, laughing, enjoying *each other*, they feel secure and can adjust to much of what life deals them. Seeing how parents interact shapes the baby's perceptions for relationships with the opposite sex, even for finding a marriage partner.

"Love Marcia," he kept repeating. "Blake will see firsthand the beauty of love. It will save him and you a lot of grief later on."

I know a young man who was conceived as a result of an extramarital affair. For nine months he heard his mother and her husband argue over whose fault this pregnancy was, and the argument continued after he was born. He wasn't wanted, and the mom and husband fought a lot. I'm no psychologist, but I think this explains a lot of the perpetual self-esteem problems that have plagued him all his life.

Josh McDowell, author and leader of a teen ministry group, says in his talks that, regardless of the true cause of marital problems, the children (babies and older) presume that they are the cause of the problems. Children of divorced parents blame themselves for the divorce and live with that guilt hanging over them the rest of their lives. Children whose parents argue a lot assume that they are the cause of this friction and that the friction will ultimately lead to divorce.

I wondered how much Blake understood when Marcia and I had a vehement discussion over the division of labor in household duties. He was sitting right in the middle of the floor, watching us intently. When the argument ended in anger and tears he was even more wide-eyed. I wondered if, in a small way, he was assuming that he had caused this conflict. Probably.

"Husbands should love their wives as they do their own bodies," Paul writes in Ephesians 5:28. In that chapter, the apostle gives fathers, husbands, wives, and children some specific advice about how to treat each other. But he includes it with advice on how members of the body of Christ should treat one another. It seems to me that the advice to the body members is meant for family members as well, since it is the extended family of God that makes up the body of Christ.

Wouldn't it change the dynamic in a lot of families, maybe our own, if we took verses 18 and beyond personally for our families? Imagine that Paul was talking to fathers about their treatment of wives and children here: "Let the Holy Spirit fill you. Speak to one another in psalms, hymns, and songs; sing and make music in your hearts to the Lord; and in the name of our Lord Jesus Christ give thanks every day for everything to our God and Father" (Eph. 5:18-20 NEB).

And what do you think would happen to arguments about household duties, responsibilities for the baby, and forgotten holidays if fathers lived this verse out in their homes: "Be subject to one another out of reverence for Christ."

When Blake was about two months old I remember getting up with him early one Saturday morning so Marcia could sleep in. I fed him, changed him, played with him, and put him back down for a nap after a couple of hours. Marcia rolled out of bed at around 11 A.M., renewed after sleeping uninterrupted for so long.

"I'd kiss your feet, but I still can't bend over," she said.

Her muscles were still sore from the pregnancy and delivery. I can afford to spend mornings like that, particularly when I bring Paul's instruction for the body into my home. Showing reverence for one another might not make my memory better about things like Mother's Day, but it should improve how the rest of our days together are spent.

Heavenly Father, forgive me when my pride and forgetfulness get in the way of my love for you and the family you have given me. Help me to see that my love for you can be shown by my love for my wife and baby.

When 'Fine' Isn't Enough

◆

Happy are those who find wisdom, . . .
her revenue is better than gold.
Proverbs 3:13-14

One of the most painful considerations about a baby is finding adequate care when both parents work. If either the mom or dad has a large enough income that the other could stay home, that would be first choice for a lot of people, including us. But in an expensive region of the country, neither Marcia's nor my salary could carry all three of us.

We felt fortunate that Marcia's company let her work part-time, and that my school gave me flexibility in coming home a lot, so we didn't need someone every day. But even for just a few days we didn't want Blake to be one of a dozen other kids who didn't get much attention. In a previous job I car-pooled with a couple who dropped their baby off at a day-care center on the way to work and picked her up on the way home. The teachers saw all of the firsts—the first bumps, the first signs of play, the first laughs, the first steps. I wondered then what the point was of having a baby when everyone but you got to be in on the joy of her development.

I understand the dilemma better now. In this country, rents and mortgage payments often demand more than what one person can produce, so another income is necessary. If a couple wants children, tough choices have to be made. Parents want to be good providers, but what is really being provided when the parents don't see their children very much?

While Marcia and I were debating our options, news magazines asked, Who's Watching the Children? Reports abounded on the difficulty couples are having in finding someone they trust to take care of their children during the day, and about concern for this generation of children raised by people other than their parents. Everywhere we looked, the issue of day care was raised. Even the comic strip "Doonsbury" was dealing with the topic during this time.

We thought the ideal situation was to have someone come to our house to take care of Blake. It was expensive, but we thought the comfort of not having to wake him up in the morning and of his remaining in familiar surroundings would be worth it. We tried for several weeks without success, then lowered our standards to taking him to the home of someone who didn't already have a houseful of kids—someone who could give him some personal attention.

We found someone like this and tried it for a few days, but were so distraught over the experience we removed him. This woman's idea of care was to set Blake in his portable chair in front of the television. Our idea was to have her play with him, help him to develop, communicate to him that the world was a good place. He didn't get that watching "Perry Mason" reruns.

At nap time she put him on his back, told him "Hush," and left the room. "He just laid there and cried, though. He just wants to be fussy," she told me. We tickle his back and hum to him until he is relaxed. No one *wants* to be fussy. He was so agitated that he wasn't sleeping or eating right. Neither were we.

After one particularly disturbing day, Marcia picked him up from the sitter's, put him in his car seat, and drove off without buckling the seat belt. At the first turn in the road he tumbled over in his seat clear across the back. Horrified, Marcia stopped the car in the middle of the street and turned him over. He laughed. She wept. We began the search again for a babysitter.

The problem was this: parents don't want a place where their baby would be merely "fine." If I had a dollar for every time I heard the phrases "He'll be fine" or "Kids are so resilient, they can put up with anything," I'd be a millionaire. No one wants to settle for "fine," or for having to make their baby "put up" with a lack of attention. Parents *like* giving their babies their undivided attention. They like caring for them. The problem is, they are the only ones who do.

No one knows your baby's different cries the way you do. Some are demands to be picked up, some are just discoveries of new noises, I suspect. But you usually know which is which. No one knows the facial expressions, the coos, the sense of play, the ways to make your baby happy, or even the different kinds of dirty diapers the way you do. It's impossible to duplicate that knowledge in others, particularly if they are caring for many children. Some parents are fortunate enough to have grandparents or other relatives nearby, so they can usually alleviate the concern for lack of attention. But for the most part it's a gamble, and I saw very few winners.

One result of this anguish was an appreciation of single parents. I still don't know how they do it. I see them with their babies in the grocery store late at night because that is the only time they have to shop. I see them struggling to get by on frazzled nerves, trying to avoid taking it out on the children. When do they get relief? When do they relax? When do they get some time to themselves? They don't. I have a new understanding of their predicament.

What we decided we needed was wisdom. We couldn't change our circumstances, and we didn't think it was right to change our standards.

"Where then does wisdom come from? And where is the place of understanding?" asks Job 28:20. It is in the fear of the Lord, according to Job and the psalmist. "The LORD by wisdom founded the earth; by understanding he established the heavens," says Proverbs 3:19.

In wisdom and understanding did God also set into motion what was right for taking care of Blake? We chose to believe that the answer was yes.

Heavenly Father, is it possible that the same wisdom that set the world in orbit is available for our predicament? You have shown your care for your children throughout humanity. We plead for your wisdom today in how to care for this tiny bead of life.

Ordering Our Days Rightly

◆

Teach us to order our days rightly.
Psalm 90:12 NEB

There are times when, in the best interest of these new creations, parents inflict pain on their babies. In the case of giving the baby a shot, it is done to avoid serious pain or disease later on in life. It's a valuable, necessary experience. But to know in advance that you are going to subject your helpless offspring to what amounts to a legal stabbing makes you an accomplice to the dreaded deed. Perhaps it's the same sensation the hangman, or the guillotine operator, or the electric chair supervisor has. He knows what's coming and when. The victim doesn't.

An additional problem with giving a baby a shot is that it is often the baby's first experience of pain. Sometimes they experience pain by accident early on—pinching fingers in car seat buckles, developing rashes on their bottoms, bumping their heads on overhead luggage compartments in airplanes, and other unplanned misfortunes. But unless they needed surgery as newborns or had one of these accidents, they don't know serious pain until the first shot. Think about what a shot is—a stranger, sometimes wearing a mask, takes a sharp foreign object and forces it through your protective shell so some stuff can get into your bloodstream. Then it leaves a little hole with blood on it, and the spot around the point of invasion swells and hurts like crazy for a few hours or days.

We know all this in advance (we even know the time!) and somehow have to deny what it looks like and go with the necessity of it. Guilt looms once again.

I wanted to be there when it happened to Blake, so we all went to the doctor's office together. We had told Blake about the shot during his bath and diaper change that morning just in case there was something in his emotional makeup that could help prepare him for the pain. It is doubtful how helpful this kind of exercise is, but it at least made us feel better that we tried to warn him.

After the doctor's exam we read about all of the possible side effects, which did nothing to settle our nerves. Not only are we going to pay someone to impale him, it also might give him seizures or kill him? What kind of parents would do that to their child? The nurse came in, holding a very small syringe, and for a fleeting moment I entertained the thought that it might not be so painful after all. The needle was so small, and her technique might be so good, that maybe it would be like the shots our dog gets, when she merely turns around and looks at the vet as if she were wondering, "Did you say something to me?" and then forgets about it.

Marcia got alongside of Blake on the table and held his hand, humming softly to keep him relaxed. The problem with that method, as I'm sure Blake will soon find out, is that when Marcia is nervous but tries to act relaxed, she hums very fast songs that aren't soothing at all. I believe she hummed the Harlem Globetrotters' theme song, "Sweet Georgia Brown," which isn't on the top ten list for songs of comfort before experiencing severe pain.

I got up by Blake's face so he could be looking at me and, hopefully, thinking about pleasant things. Then the nurse said, "A little stick now," and did the deed. Blake froze for a moment, looked directly at Marcia, then at me, and burst into screams.

There. We did it. We introduced him to pain. All of us in the room were crying in a matter of seconds. In about 15 minutes he calmed down and fell asleep on the way to the car. Later I called from work to see how he was, and Marcia said that he was either sleeping or screaming, and that she would be doing the same if I came home late.

It was important for me to be there for this shot, because I'm so bound to all of this newness. I wanted to be there as a comfort to Blake, but I also wanted to see what this new sensation would be like. Having a baby means you get to see everything all over again, but at a distance.

When Blake screamed, so did my insides. I experienced the pain with him, wanted to comfort him, wanted to take the pain away, wanted to convince him that his dad would make it all better and that he was in safe hands.

Not every father can do this, of course. Some don't have the flexibility in schedule to go to their own doctor's appointment, let alone one for their child. Some don't see the need. Fathers, though, need to be in on at least *some* firsts with their babies, in my opinion. The babies need to get the message that they are a shared being, that mom *and* dad take these things seriously and that both can be part of the comfort.

One of my elderly colleagues, who has three grown children, proclaimed with great pride to me that he had never changed a diaper in his life. He probably also never got to experience the intangibles of being face-to-face when his babies were at their most vulnerable moments. He didn't get those gazes. Those moments communicate a lot of love.

What bothers me about missing these opportunities of closeness is not that the babies miss out on them, but that the fathers do. Those moments change us. They make us vulnerable. They make us hurt and laugh with our children. The experience is a shared one that bonds the baby to the new creature the baby created in us—the father. And that bonding should occur sooner than later.

"Teach us to order our days rightly, that we may enter the gate of wisdom" (Psalm 90:12 NEB). As fathers, ordering our days rightly should include making time to share these moments whenever possible. Starting now.

Our Father, you know us so well that you share in our joys and hurts. Give us the wisdom and time to know our children as well as you know us.

The Value of a Parenting Style

◆

With what shall I come before the L*ORD?*

Micah 6:6

We like to think there is a lot of purity involved in parenting, so we often don't admit that, when other parents pass us in the store, we check out the brand of the stroller or notice whether the child is dressed as handsomely as ours. The great passive put-down is, "We looked at those, but decided we liked these better." It can refer to anything—brands of clothes, types of car seat, or nighttime tapes. Just as we do with one another as adults, we like to compare ourselves as parents to one another.

Nowhere is this more evident than when it comes to parenting styles. Now that I'm a parent I find myself assessing the parenting of others, based entirely on the notion, "Do they do it the way I do it?"

Somehow parents and grandparents make up their minds that there is a certain age when things should or shouldn't be happening anymore. I've heard these comments from one parent to another several times: "She's *still* on a bottle?" "You *never* breastfed him?" "You're *still* breastfeeding him?" "He's not potty-trained *yet*?" "She's *still* sucking her thumb?" "He doesn't go to bed until 10?"

Ingrained in each of these is the judgment that someone other than the actual parents has superior knowledge. Sometimes someone does. I had that feeling when I saw one crawling baby in our church nursery bite another one so hard on the cheek that she drew blood. I had a similar feeling when, on a crowded airplane, I saw a mom breastfeed her ten-year-old boy while he stood in the aisle. But parents and grandparents do a lot of comparing and judging of each other on more minor things than endangering others or breastfeeding an adolescent. And each one believes that the parenting style adopted in his or her home is the right one for everyone.

At a friend's house I got to see three distinct parenting styles among the three dads whose families were there for dinner. We all had our babies with us in the living room as we tried to discuss an important issue. One dad took the laissez-faire approach, and his fifteen-month-old boy viewed any flat surface as a challenge for him to clear off and stand upon. The result was a few broken candles, swept off the coffee table in the middle of the room.

"Well, they must not be very important items to have been left out like that," was the dad's response. It wasn't his house, nor were they his candles. But it *was* his child.

The other dad was gracious and participated in the conversation to a point, but was always checking on where his baby girl was crawling off to and retrieving her. My style was to hover. Everything was potentially life-threatening in my view—especially the laissez-faire dad's boy.

After a while the other boy took to screaming. He threw his dinner into three different rooms in a matter of seconds, making passage on the hardwood floors a delicate task. He then clubbed the little girl with a wooden spoon until she, too, was screaming. The boy's dad didn't get out of his chair but offered a feeble, "Buddy, no, no." The boy's mom came into the room and she, too, seemed unable to deal with the crisis.

"I'm vanquished," she sighed. She said she had not had a decent night's sleep since a few months before the boy was born. That makes about two years. Even before he was born this kid was running the house.

"We have declared him the winner," the dad concurred over the screaming. "Our paws are in the air." At fifteen months, the baby is the ruler in that family.

Actually, the baby in our family is ruler also, but it isn't the tyranny in ours it is in theirs. Blake is more of a benevolent dictator. Our world still revolves around him, and we arrange our lives to take care of his needs. But he's not like Mussolini, the way that other baby is, a person who will punish those who don't obey. Somehow that family needs a coup to overthrow the present power structure.

My dad has said for years that when people have babies, they treat them as if they are the center of the universe for the first three years or so, then spend the next thirty years trying to convince them that they are no longer the center of the universe. I understand that now. Except in this family's case I guess the former message was a little too convincing. Many Native Americans view life as a circle, and we, babies included, are part of the circle—no one is ever in the center.

The issue, though, is that we pass judgment on one another all the time, based on our perceptions of what "good parenting" is. I know people who think Marcia and I hover too much, that we are too hesitant about leaving Blake with strangers at the nursery or with baby-sitters.

What, ultimately, do we want to happen as a result of our parenting? Don't we want for our sons and daughters the same things God wants for his sons and daughters on earth? And what does God want from us? That we do justice, love kindness, and walk humbly with our God (Micah 6:8). That we love God with our heart, soul, strength, and mind; and love our neighbor as ourself (Luke 10:27). Isn't that really what we want for our own children?

When I come to this conclusion, I am less concerned about how late other parents let their kids stay up, or how long they let them use a bottle. A bigger issue I want to confront as a parent today is whether I am providing an atmosphere for Blake to want to love God. The style becomes less important than the objective.

> *Create in me, O Father, a dad whose love points the way to you. Help me to see that this is my true purpose in being a dad.*

Before Pride There Is Wonder

◆

And he took them up his arms,
laid his hands on them,
and blessed them.
Mark 10:16

Fathers love to talk about their kids. This is not a revolutionary thought—we've all heard fathers brag about how hard their kids can kick a soccer ball or how early in life they could read. By listening to one of my colleagues where I teach, one could surmise that major league baseball will have to salivate for four more years as it waits for his son to pitch for them.

But fathers don't talk that way about their *babies*. Talking about their babies doesn't draw out the machismo the way talking about ten-year-olds can. When fathers talk about their ten-year-olds, their voices are filled with pride. When fathers talk about their babies, their voices are filled with wonder.

"I look at my sleeping babies and think they represent innocence in its purest form," one father told me. "Nothing bad should ever happen to them. If something bad happens to you or me, it's probably tolerable and we probably had it coming. But the children—they ought to be raised where the world is a friendly place."

That's exactly how I feel about Blake. He came to this world by invitation. Carrying him against my shoulder one day, I stopped in front of a mirror and got to watch him fall asleep. It was a calming, moving experience. He is simply a picture of purity. When he is happy, he is pure joy. When he is upset, he is pure need. Asleep, he is tear-inducing innocence.

When Blake was a few weeks old I got a letter of congratulation from a friend who sells insurance in Minnesota. He has two boys. "I can still remember going out to a business meeting and being the only guy who had a blotch of thrown-up milk on my shoulder," he wrote. "After living with a three- and five-year-old, I've decided that God does exist and I think he's even got a pretty good plan.

"We get these helpless, adorable little things called babies, and they really are quite irresistible. They cry and smile and coo, etc.; all the while they are growing on you. Then they turn three. Suddenly they are smarter than you are and have you right where they want you. Your problem is, it's too late. You like them by now.

"If boys were three when born, you'd kill them immediately.

"We're happy for you. Teach him to skate with his head up when he's playing hockey."

One father, a basketball buddy, always gets a certain gleam in his eye when he talks about the baby in his house. This one is his fourth. We were in a restaurant when he asked how my days as a new father were going. Specifically, he asked how proficient I was at changing diapers. I told him that I was competent, but that we were using cloth diapers and I could never get them tight enough around Blake's legs. I kept finding surprises in his socks because of my loose fittings.

This dad took great pleasure in giving me a demonstration, using a napkin and a salad plate, of a surefire way to do it. He swelled in a fatherly way, much to the amusement of the other restaurant guests.

A couple of years ago I was in southern Mexico on a writing assignment, and one of the Americans I was with got word that his two-month-old baby had pneumonia and was under an oxygen tent in an Oklahoma hospital. My colleague didn't hesitate to speed back to the States. Not being a father at the time, I was surprised at his haste. The boy's life was not in danger, so couldn't we finish the assignment? I asked. He said the thought of that helpless, uncomprehending life with tubes sticking out of him, without his dad by his side, was too much.

"As much capacity as there is for them to bring joy into your life, there is an equal capacity and intensity to feel the other emotions, too," he said. "I can't deal with not being there."

We got someone to drive him to Mexico City so he could try to get a flight out. Close to the airport the van got a flat tire. He helped push the van to a gas station, grabbed his suitcase, and ran the final mile in scorching heat.

Not everyone feels this way about kids, though. In the newspaper recently was a story about a war between two Middle Eastern countries. To sweep the area for mines before sending their troops, they sent their children wearing headbands that said "To God." If there were mines, the kids were blown up to heaven. I guess innocence has value in war, too.

The innocence that we find so attractive in our children is the same kind of innocence God asks of us when we approach him. "Whoever does not receive the kingdom of God as a little child will never enter it," Jesus said in Mark 10:15. We can learn something about God by seeing how our children look at us and then imitating them. Equally exciting in that incident in Mark is Jesus' response to the children around him. As a father, I understand the response even better: he put his arms around them.

My associate in Mexico knew that his son didn't understand pain but would feel better with his father near by. That strikes me as a reasonable sentiment now. If something happened to Blake, I would do the same—only I might not stop to tell my friends good-bye.

Father in heaven, you look at us the way we look at our children. Help us to look to you the way our children look to us.

When the Future Doesn't Include Us

◆

Life is more than food,
and the body more than clothing.
Luke 12:23

Unless we have a terminal disease, most of us don't spend a lot of time thinking about how we want things to be after we are gone, because we don't think much about being taken out of this world before we're old.

We leave windows open in the house because we'll be back pretty soon—how much damage can a burglar or rainstorm do in an hour? We have answering machines for our phones so we can return calls when we get back—of course we'll be back. Appliances with a one-year guarantee are more attractive than those with a one-month guarantee because we presume we will be around for at least the year. We are told not only what check-*in* time is at a hotel, but also the check-*out* time, because everyone assumes we will survive the night. We almost always buy round-trip tickets.

Two things prompted a "What if I die soon?" discussion between Marcia and me, particularly as it related to taking care of Blake in the absence of the other. The first incident was a visit from a mom with her five-year-old boy. The dad, distracted by his career and complex personality, chose not to be burdened with being an involved dad, so the mom is pretty much a single parent. She didn't seem bitter about it—just resigned to the knowledge that whatever development she wants to occur in her son is her responsibility. This has resulted in some pretty compulsive behavior. She says she constantly fights the urge to say, "This is still painting time. Reading time isn't for another 20 minutes," instead of just letting her kid have this one chance to be a kid.

I took the boy to our yard, hoping to see what being a father would be like five years from now. I got out a plastic bat and ball and tried to play with him, but it was clear that there had been no influence in this regard. I should have been satisfied that, because of his mom's influence, he knew all about the Library of Congress, but I was still appalled that he was afraid a slow-moving plastic ball would hurt him. When he threw, the ball went straight into the ground in front of him. I taught him the best I could, but he lost interest and we went back inside.

The other incident was having dinner with two high school girls Marcia and I babysat for ten years ago. Their dad and I had collaborated on a book called *God Never Said You'd Be Leading at the Half*, and I loved that family dearly. In a tragic accident their dad died the year the book came out, while they were nine or ten. I hadn't seen the girls for a few years, so when I was in their city on business, I called them. As a new father I viewed the loss of their dad in a new light. Their father was an excellent dad, in my opinion. He was involved in his girls' lives, a good provider and a wonderful role model.

There was one thing he couldn't provide, though—a replacement. His control and direction for the family ended when he died. The mom remarried, but life at home was rough with the new husband. I felt helpless and frustrated listening to how their lives had gone in the years since their dad died. I was also fearful because it made me consider what life would be like for Blake if I didn't make it home one night.

I *want* to be an influence in his life. I *want* to be a role model for him. I *want* to be the one he calls when he's in trouble or hurting or confused. I presume I will be all of those things, but I began to consider what needed to occur in his life should I not be here.

That's when Marcia and I had our contingency talk. We agreed that we wanted Blake to continue to be brought up in an atmosphere where people believed in having a personal walk with Christ, so that when it was time for him to choose, he would have seen the difference Christ makes in people's lives. We wanted him to go to college (an attainable goal to achieve with a new insurance policy). We wanted him to respect the sanctity of life—human and otherwise.

"Indulge me," I said to Marcia. These platitudes were important, but I needed to get something off my chest. "Please don't let him get to age five without his knowing how to catch, throw, and hit a ball." I don't know precisely why this was important, but it was. "I can't bear to watch from my angelic perch while he goes to school and the kids make fun of him for not knowing some playground fundamentals."

He needed to get over the fear of a descending football and he needed to know how to skate and stickhandle a puck without looking at the ice.

Marcia stopped me there. "And how do you expect me to teach him that?"

"Marry another hockey player." I didn't care if he wasn't a star. I just wanted him to hold his own.

Then it was Marcia's turn for final requests. "Make sure that after you bathe him, you clean under his fingernails. He looks like a car mechanic after you bathe him." I believed I could remember that. "Go to him when he cries out in the night, regardless of what the books say about teaching him to quiet himself. If his mom is gone, he'll need you."

This led to a discussion about choosing a guardian for him if both of us should die. Do we go with a couple whose lifestyle looks fun, or do we go with the more stable and boring? We didn't settle that one for a long time.

It is a simple thing to say we will leave it in God's hands, but that doesn't take away the responsibility of good planning if we are able. Is planning the opposite of faith? Can it be overdone? The list of what to turn over to the caring, eternal hands of the Father continues to grow.

You have said you would be the Father to the fatherless, dear Lord, and I believe you. I give my family's future to you today.

Like Father, Like Son

◆

The children of a family share
the same flesh and blood;
and so he too shared ours . . .
Hebrews 2:14 NEB

As a baseball fan I enjoy watching the outfielder Ken Griffey Jr. play, comparing his style to his father's, who also played in the major leagues. I think the younger Griffey has a stronger arm, but the older one could hit better. I also like to watch the hockey player Brett Hull, who alone usually scores more goals than most teams do. I grew up watching his dad Bobby play pro hockey, and I get a kick out of seeing some of the same moves. Brett takes less time to shoot and is more accurate, but his dad could shatter the plexiglass behind the net with the velocity of his shot.

There are certain traits about our own fathers that we embrace. If our fathers were kind, helpful people and we find ourselves being kind and helpful, there is comfort in assuming that those characteristics were passed from one generation to the next. If our fathers were artistically or athletically inclined and we have a gift in those areas, too, then we credit them with passing the gifts down the line.

My wife can say, "You looked just like your dad when you did that," and it can make me feel good. There is a patient and compassionate side to him that I hope has been passed down to me. Not all of his traits are desirable, though. If my wife tells me I remind her of my dad while I'm driving, that means either I'm driving so slowly that an Amish buggy could zip past, or that I found a parking spot that is the farthest possible distance from our destination.

If we do things that remind others of our parents, it is natural to wonder what things our babies will do that are similar to the way we do them. Even things like whether they cry, eat, sleep, or laugh the way we do is important information because that's all they do right now.

Perhaps we wonder about these things because we *really* wonder if they will have our traits later in life. Will they, like us, jump to conclusions, get fat just walking past chocolate, snore, have a short temper, drive like a maniac, spell poorly? Is there anything we can do to keep some of those traits from recurring in this new generation?

My mom came out for a visit shortly after Blake was born, and I was anxious to find out what he did that was like me. He had a deep guffaw for a laugh, and I wondered if he got that from me. He also had an intense stare when he looked at people and that made them feel uncomfortable, as if he was trying to read their minds. It was almost as if he despised them for coming into his line of vision.

He also had a tremendous capacity for burping. He once burped so loudly that I thought a rhinoceros had snuck into the house, let go of a war cry, and escaped. Blake would often wait until the last minute for this eruption, so that meant we were cleaning milk off of each other and the ceiling if he waited too long.

I suspect he got this from my side of the family because I have distinct memories of being at the dinner table with my two brothers, and my oldest brother getting through most of the Gettysburg Address in one long explosion. It isn't easy, or pretty, and I still can't do it, but I know it is in my family genes. Marcia's family would not have contributed this trait because they felt that burping was something that only uncivilized, primitive people were capable of doing.

After several days of studying Blake's every move, my mom could find few similarities. "He doesn't look like anyone I know," she said.

There are a few things I hope he does get from me, and a few I hope he gets from Marcia. I hope he likes to read. I hope he likes sports but not so much that they consume him (and if they do consume him I hope he excels in one of them and makes a bazillion dollars so his parents can retire in Hawaii). I hope he gets the spiritual sensitivity of his mother. She can be in tune with someone's need halfway around the globe and know what to do about it. I hope he is capable of looking people in the eye and listening to them about what interests them or concerns them. I hope he loves God.

There are also some characteristics of mine I hope he doesn't adopt. I hope he has an easier time with authority than I did as a boy and young man. I hope he communicates his feelings to God, his wife, and his parents better than I did. It will save him a lot of pain if he can get hold of that early. At the same time, I hope he isn't swayed by his emotions as much as I was when I was young.

What I really hope is that he takes on the characteristics of Christ as his own. And as we read in Scripture, the characteristics of Christ are those of God, and Christ promises us God's Spirit in John 14:26 as a way to keep those characteristics alive. "The Advocate, the Holy Spirit, whom the Father will send in my name, will teach you everything, and remind you of all that I have said to you," Jesus tells us.

It's one thing to have someone say, "You remind me of your dad." It is something else to have someone say, "You remind me of Christ." In some ways I hope Blake does remind people of me. In other ways he would be better off if he didn't. But my dream is to have a child who reminds people of Christ. The Holy Spirit is here to make it happen.

Father, it isn't just a lofty goal to try to be like you. You make it possible when we look to you. Help us, as we bring up our children, to train them to look to you so the world will see more of your traits and fewer of ours.

On Loan from God

◆

Samuel continued in the service of the Lord.

1 Samuel 2:18 NEB

One of the more tender moments of a church service is when children are baptized or dedicated to God. It helps us as parents to focus on what we really want to happen with our babies. We want them given to God because they are really on loan to us from God. We may spend a lot of years forgetting that fact, but at least for this moment we acknowledge whose children these really are.

The example of Hannah and her son Samuel takes the idea of dedication to a new level. After being filled with grief that she hadn't borne any children, she poured herself out before God, and soon after God gave her Samuel. When Samuel was a little boy she brought him to the temple and left him in the care of the priest Eli. Since Samuel had been an answer to her prayer, she gave him to the priest to serve God. Now *that's* dedicating your little one to God!

The modern-day parallel, perhaps, is what parents do when they want their little ones to be gymnasts in the Olympics. They send them off to the coach's house for months or years and hope to see them occasionally. The result is muscular, agile, extremely competitive, and focused young people.

My parents sent me away to Boy Scout camp for two weeks every summer so that I would learn how to live in the woods, in a tent with other tenderfeet, under a cloud of mosquitoes that could suck an ox dry in a minute, with a Scout leader who would vomit at the first sign of stress. He was bent over a lot those two weeks. We learned a lot about survival, got real dirty, and went back home to a normal life.

But a camp is different from sending a little one away for an extended time for a stated purpose, with an occasional visit from mom and dad. Most of us won't send our kids away for most of their childhood so they can become super athletes or priests or campers. What we often do instead is make a public confession with our babies that we want them to be God's throughout their lives. We want to give them proper instruction and create a proper atmosphere in the home so the children will eventually develop their own relationship with God and serve him throughout their lives. Some churches also have the congregation participate in the dedication or baptism service by reading a statement about how they, too, will do what they can to bring this baby up in service to God.

We had a dedication/baptism service for Blake when he was four months old, at a family reunion in upstate New York. The chapel was empty except for our family, so we created a circle of people on the platform. Symbolically it was the right thing because now he was part of that circle of family, and we all served as influences on one another. We read the story of Hannah giving Samuel to Eli. For a fleeting moment I think I felt a little of what she felt—so much gratitude to God for giving her this tiny gift that her purest response was to give him back to God. That's what we were doing, too. We knew that day that Blake was God's and that we were his caretakers for a few years. We knew that it was only a matter of time before we were not his caretakers any longer, and that he would be making his own decisions about God, about his role in society, about his priorities.

We wanted God's blessing on us as parents, on the others as cousins, aunts, uncles, and grandparents. We were charged that day with the knowledge that it was our job to bring Blake up in service to God for the brief time that we had him.

I am not under the illusion that this means Blake will become a pastor or missionary or adopt some other traditional calling for those who serve God. I'm a journalist and a teacher. Marcia is an accountant. We both serve God. We hope Blake will, too, regardless of his stated career. We can't all be priests, but we can all be disciples.

I was talking with a dad of two boys, ages seven and ten, and I asked him what he tells his guys about serving God. One can't decide whether to be a pilot, an actor, or a doctor. The other wants to play professional baseball.

"We don't talk much about being pastors or missionaries," the dad said. "If that's what they're going to be, God will get that message to them. What we talk about is being spiritual leaders.

"When we pray we ask that they will be the kind of people others look to because it is so obvious they know God and serve him." It is a similar prayer to Hannah's.

I like the thought of having a son people look to because it is so obvious he knows God. My grandparents were that way. People who knew them would say to me, "You're Paul and Naomi Cunningham's grandson? They really knew the Lord." Then they would tell stories of how my grandparents took them in, or stayed with them during a crisis, or prayed with them, or provided insight into God's Word, or showed spiritual discernment when it came to tough choices. Their life-style pointed people to God, wherever they lived and whatever their occupation. God used them in miraculous ways. That's one of the reasons Blake's middle name is Cunningham. We want God to use him.

"As Samuel grew up, the LORD was with him and let none of his words fall to the ground. And all Israel from Dan to Beersheba knew that Samuel was a trustworthy prophet of the LORD," says 1 Samuel 3:19-20.

Ultimately the choice about whether God uses Blake will be Blake's. For now, though, I have a role model in Hannah, a parent who could see who Samuel really belonged to. As a prayer of faith we could all substitute our children's names for Samuel's in 1 Samuel 2:21: "The boy Samuel grew up in the presence of the LORD."

Father, we will spend the rest of our lives rededicating our children to you. At the beginning of these lives, though, we want them, and us, to be in your service. May our children grow up in the presence of the Lord.

Sharing the Right Now

◆

See, I am making all things new.
Revelation 21:5

Dads like to do things with their kids long before the kids have any lasting idea of the value or fun of the experience. It's a safe assumption that my son will not remember going hiking in the San Jacinto mountains in southern California. He slept most of the time in the front pack. It is doubtful he will remember going to Minnesota for the World Series.

Yet, on days when I was the one home alone with him, I liked the idea of going someplace special each day. I would scour the newspaper for events or sights that he might enjoy. The Clydesdale horses were at a local shopping mall one day, and I took him there. He stared intently at them for a long time, and they stared at him. I don't know what I was expecting, since he barely notices our German shepherd dog at home.

I take him to the San Diego bay frequently just to look at the boats. Why do I point out certain kinds of boats and explain to him what they do? He can't understand English. He's been on the planet for just a few months and I want him to comprehend that Clydesdales are unusually big horses and that aircraft carriers can hold up to 12,000 people at sea.

One of those trips to the bay will be memorable, I suspect, if he is ever put under hypnosis later in life. After walking out on a pier with him and describing the different kinds of fish the fishermen had brought in, I put him back in his stroller. For some reason I couldn't get the stroller handle to lock, and when Blake finally screamed in a manner that raised the fish from the dead, I saw that his fingers were caught in the lock mechanism. For the most part, though, I provided interesting and enjoyable experiences for him.

But why should we do these things when we know the babies won't remember them? Do we have a purpose beyond just passing the time or to get out of the house? I think so. Taking our babies to places we think are fun or special is a way to begin our lives as a shared experience. Taking Blake to see horses or boats is a way to let him in on what his dad thinks is fun.

This was especially true on a day when I was one of the organizers for some faculty meetings at the beginning of the school year. For the sports junkies on the faculty there is a tradition that, at the end of the meeting, we go to the gym to play basketball. It was my day to be at home with Blake, but since I also had this commitment I took him with me. A student played with him during the morning, and when it was time for hoops I took him to the gym. As luck would have it, there were nine guys—perfect for four-on-four with one substitution. At their insistence (I'm serious), the person who rotated out would watch Blake.

It was fun to get to play in the game, of course, but it was just as much fun seeing Blake on the floor in the gym corner, giggling uncontrollably at having a basketball rolled to him by one of my colleagues. After the game I took a quick shower and came out to a wonderful sight. Blake was sound asleep against the disgustingly sweaty chest of the 6′8″ basketball coach. Both were happy as clams.

When we got back to the house, Marcia was home. She picked him up and made a sour face. "Where has he been? He smells terrible," she said. I proudly explained that he had been held and played with by nine sweaty basketball players and had probably nearly drowned in the center's shirt. It was an exciting day, I told her. She went directly to the bathroom with him and gave him an extended bath.

As much joy as there is in these shared experiences, there is an equal amount of emptiness on days so busy that dads don't see their babies at all. There's not much shared experience when I have to leave for work before Blake wakes up, and I get home about a half hour before he goes to bed, or sometimes after he goes to bed. Everyone is the loser in that kind of day because Marcia gets no relief from taking care of him all day, he gets no interaction with me, and I don't get to see the subtle changes that occur every day.

When evening meetings go on longer than they should (which is most of them), I find myself looking at my watch, hoping that I get out of this discussion in time to at least put Blake to bed. One particular night I was more irritated than usual by an endless meeting, and I drove home quickly, knowing that it was way beyond Blake's bedtime. It felt good to drive home fast anyway. Marcia anticipated this, though, and kept Blake up so that I could hold him at least once that day. He was tired and crabby. So was I. The two of us walked around the house, listened to his favorite country music album, and calmed down together. He fell asleep on my shoulder, and I felt as if those moments were the most significant part of my day.

It is the shared experience that brings so much joy in our lives as parents. Not having a shared experience leaves my day empty, regardless of what I accomplished at work. With some circumstances, this is unavoidable, though. When I travel, I miss out on a lot.

I have a new appreciation for the right now, since I have been taking care of this growing, dependent, continuously changing life. As Christians we are brought up to take the long view on things—trials may endure for the night, but joy comes in the morning, for instance. Our sufferings are only temporary—we will spend eternity with God in heaven. But there is joy right now, too, in sharing a moment that has never been experienced before, and you're both a little different as a result. In his poem, "Auguries of Innocence," William Blake wrote,

To see a world in a grain of sand,
And a heaven in a wild flower—
Hold infinity in the palm of your hand,
And eternity in an hour.

These shared moments are chances to hold eternity in an hour.

Heavenly Father, there is so much to experience with this new life. Help me to plan wisely for his future, but help me to see the joy of life together right now, too.

The Protective Parent

◆

Guard the good treasure entrusted to you,
with the help of the Holy Spirit
living in us.
2 Timothy 1:14

As previously mentioned, new parents take stock of their surroundings. They look to see if things are nice enough and clean enough for the new baby. But they also have a new perspective on whether things are safe enough.

Moments after reading an article about babies being asphyxiated in house fires, poisoning themselves with chemicals found in cabinets under kitchen sinks, and drowning by falling into toilets, Marcia went on a safety-latch binge. She brought home a sackful of smoke alarms and devices designed to keep curious, crawling babies out of things behind doors and lids. Unfortunately, they kept hungry, irritated adults out of them, too. The package showed a slender housewife easily dismantling the things with one manicured hand, but I had to forcefully squeeze with one hand and pull with the other to have even a 50-50 chance of getting the doors open again. When I threatened to leave a hacksaw or bolt cutters on the counter, I was informed that then the kitchen would be less safe than it was without the locks. You should have seen us wrestle with the latch on the toilet seat. It wasn't a pretty picture.

We take risks in our adult lives because we know we can handle the consequences. For months I drove on tires that were so bald that the steel belts wore through and they created sparks as I drove on the highway. If they went flat, I reasoned, I could negotiate the car to the side of the road, call a tow truck, buy new tires, and be on my way, delayed by only a few hours.

I would never consider driving on tires like that now. The prospect of standing at the side of a highway, holding a baby who is screaming for his mother, who is fearful of the traffic noise, and who knows that his dad could have avoided this stupid predicament, is one I didn't want to face.

Likewise, Marcia and I reevaluated our MG Midget. It was a fun car to drive, but it broke down often and we knew that we would only have one accident with it, and we would lose. Did we want to drive that car with a new baby in it, knowing that we would have no chance in a confrontation with another car? We sold it and bought a Volvo. I predict I'll be driving a sports car again one day, but now is not the time.

Smoke alarms, cabinet latches, tires, and cars are things we can control. It tests the mettle of a parent to see how many dangers out there are outside of our control.

Every state has its own unique set of natural disasters—tornadoes, floods, blizzards. The first earthquake my wife and I encountered in California was almost amusing—as, if our bed was a giant surfboard and we were riding the crest of the wave across the room. The first earthquake we felt after Blake was born had us flying to his room and leaning over his bed to protect him from any falling objects. Nothing fell and he didn't wake up, but the incident brought out awareness in us that some things are more than a matter of good preparation.

My most frightening moment in Blake's first few months occurred at the beach. I did all the right parenting things to protect him, I thought: I had enough sunblock to cover an elephant, a broad-brimmed hat, a spray bottle to squirt sand out of his eyes, and an umbrella that stuck in the sand so we could play in the shade.

After crawling around and digging for a while, we sat by the edge of the water, letting the waves come in and wash over our legs. An unusually large wave rolled in and hit me at chest level, well above Blake's head, and in a flash he was gone. I couldn't see him or feel him. When I jumped up I saw his hat on top of the water about five feet from me. I lunged for it and it was still attached to Blake. I grabbed him out of the water and ran back to our blanket, praying with my entire being that he was okay. When I got him under the umbrella he sputtered and waved his arms and made ugly faces at the taste of the salt water, but he was okay. He looked around, not crying, and crawled back toward the water. I thought I was going to have a heart attack.

The earthquake and the wave showed me how unpredictable things are and how quickly everything can change, regardless of the planning we do. The back of our car is a virtual mobile bomb shelter. But you can't plan for everything when trying to protect yourself or your children.

When I worked on an ambulance crew I was dispatched to a house where a two-year-old had stopped breathing. The boy was born with cancer and battled courageously, but he lost the fight. He died before we got there. I chatted briefly with the mom before we took the little body away—I was a well-meaning college kid who knew nothing about this kind of pain. The cancer wasn't a result of bad planning or carelessness. No one else in the family had it. She was both enraged and despondent. I wish I could tell her that, nearly twenty years later, I think I'm closer to understanding her grief and confusion.

When the psalmist tells us that we who put our trust in the Lord will live under his shelter and that we will find safety in

God, does it mean physical safety for our children, too? I wish it did. I do know that there is truth in the psalms, "For you, the Lord is a safe retreat; you have made the Most High your refuge" (Psalm 91:9 NEB). Even when there is no assurance of safety, there is assurance of rest.

I want to be a dad who keeps harmful chemicals, cars, tires, germs, and waves away from my baby. And I want to be a follower of God who chooses God as a refuge when I am reminded of how many things are out of my control.

Dear Lord, our refuge, thank you for giving us the desire to protect our children. Amid our responsibility, though, show us the safety you provide for us beneath your wings.

When the Father Is Also a Child

◆

God is treating you as children.
Hebrews 12:7

When we were young, we probably had mixed reactions when Jesus referred to God as "our Father." When I heard the metaphor in Sunday school it didn't register with me as a problem because I had such a good experience with my own father. Hearing God referred to as a father meant, to me, that he must be loving, disciplining (but not with a huge authority complex), sacrificing, and involved in my daily life. If God was like that, or more, then that was fine with me, because that's what I experienced with my father.

Later in life I found out that the metaphor wasn't as meaningful to others. Their own experiences with their fathers were such that considering God as an extension of that relationship was quite frightening. A professional pianist I know was made to lean over her piano bench while her father spanked her. The very object of her desire and ability became a prop for her dad to hit her. A business manager I know was, as a youngster, struck repeatedly in the face with a shoe by his alcoholic father. A student at the college where I teach was made to perform humiliating sexual acts for her father. For these people and others like them, the thought of God being like their fathers was not very attractive.

Their fathers were unreasonable, abusive disciplinarians who did not allow questioning and exercised authority for the sake of domination and power. If God was an extension of that behavior, then they didn't see much reason to enter into a relationship with him.

There is a new perspective on the metaphor of God the Father, though, to those of us who are new fathers. Instead of relating God the Father to the kind of fathers we had, we now relate God the Father to the kind of fathers we want to be.

We find ourselves disciplining our little ones—even at this early age—because we know it will help them in the long run. It is painful for them *and us*, yet we know that if we don't insist in some areas, there will be problems later. For instance, Blake likes to be held until he falls asleep. Frankly, I like that practice as well. It feels wonderful to sense him relaxing, then completely dropping off while being held against my neck or shoulder. But everything we read and hear says that if he doesn't learn to put himself to sleep in bed, we'll be holding him until he's ready for college.

So we get him calm, play his favorite country music album, then lay him in bed. He cries immediately, of course, because that's not what he wants. The second he's down he pops his head up, rolls on his back, and cries. We leave the room, let him cry for about five minutes, then go back in and do it all over again. This can go on for about forty minutes before he finally drops off, and I feel bad that he falls asleep with disappointment or sadness as his last conscious thought. It's painful, but necessary, for him to learn this.

I'm reading Hebrews 12:5-6 with a new perspective these days. I used to read it as a person receiving discipline, from the perspective of one who has a father. Now I also read it as a person giving discipline, from the perspective of one who *is* a father.

> *"My child, do not regard lightly the discipline of the Lord,*
> *or lose heart when you are punished by him;*
> *for the Lord disciplines those whom he loves."*

Now I compare myself as the father to God the Father. It's a new concept.

When I am home with Blake he depends on me for everything. Whether he eats, sleeps, or is clean is up to me. I am his ultimate provider, and he trusts me completely. Without my caring for his needs he would suffer greatly. What's more, I *like* doing these things for Blake. I delight in making him happy. If he's having fun, then I'm having fun. When he's awake I concentrate not only on meeting his needs, but also on helping him enjoy himself. When he's asleep, I get things ready for him so that his waking hours are more enjoyable.

It sounds like what God wants to do for us, doesn't it? When I am doing what I think is best for my son, which can include making him temporarily unhappy, and when I delight in his delight, and when I work to make his life smoother and happier even when he is unable to comprehend what I am doing, I think I am doing what God the Father continually does for us. As a new father who is virtually consumed with providing for his child, I have a clearer picture of the nature of God and why Jesus uses the metaphor of God the Father.

But because I have a little one who depends on me, I also have a clearer picture of what it means to be a child of God. When Jesus says in Matthew 18:3-4, "Unless you change and become like children, you will never enter the kingdom of heaven. Whoever becomes humble like this child is the greatest in the kingdom of heaven," he is telling the disciples that they need to look to God the way they used to look to their fathers when they were children. I need to trust, cry out to, cling to, depend on, and accept discipline from God the way Blake does with me.

Where does Christian maturity fit in, then? The similarity between our spiritual maturing and our children's maturing ends here. My dad doesn't provide for me anymore, nor does he discipline me. I don't depend on him as I used to because I grew up and became self-sufficient. But Jesus says we need to reconsider our spiritual self-sufficiency and return to a child-like faith in him, not as babies, but as simple, humble believers who come to God as they would a loving Father.

I want to be that kind of child. And I want to be that kind of father.

Heavenly Father, thank you for giving us direction on what kind of children to be and what kind of fathers to be. Please give us the power to be both today.

Having the Right Stuff

◆

They are to do good, to be rich in good works,
generous, and ready to share,
thus storing up for themselves the treasure of
a good foundation for the future.
1 Timothy 6:18-19

After a peaceful experience of putting my son to bed one evening and knowing that he would be asleep for the next several hours, I spread out a stack of papers on the kitchen table, ready to do a few hours' work. I knew there would be no interruption because Marcia was at her office, working late, Blake was asleep, and the phone was turned off. The only light on was the one above the kitchen table.

The silence of the evening was broken suddenly by a voice I had never heard before saying, "Alex, it's time to go to bed now." Not only had I never heard this voice before, I also had never met anyone named Alex. "Come on, Alex, let's go," the voice said. It was coming from inside my house, which, unfortunately, was pitch black except for the light above the kitchen table.

My primal paternal instincts sent me quickly down the hall to Blake's room where I hesitated for a moment, then burst in to make sure he was safe. He was sound asleep, and there was no one else in there. I went on a room-to-room search and found nothing. Except the voice. It was like a scene out of a Stephen King novel. "It's time for bed." Everywhere I walked I could hear it. "Alex, I don't want to tell you again." But it didn't belong to anyone in the house.

I finally went to the kitchen window in case the mystery voice was in the yard. The voice was immediately under my chin. "It's getting late." I looked down and saw the monitor we have on the counter. One half is in Blake's room and the other is in the kitchen so we can hear if he is crying. The voice was coming from Blake's monitor, but the voice wasn't in Blake's room. I double-checked. All I could figure was that the monitors operate on a frequency like a radio, and someone was using another monitor that had the same frequency as ours. I went from being afraid to amused in about a second. A polite person probably would have been embarrassed to invade someone's privacy like this and turned the appliance off. I listened as the voice read Alex a bedtime story, and as Alex asked for a glass of water before going to bed.

Then my imagination went wild. What if I overhear a plot to smuggle drugs or guns or endangered toucans across the border? What if I hear plans to blow up the Pentagon? How would we find the smugglers/terrorists?

While I was eavesdropping and imagining, Marcia came home and saw me hovering over the monitor. "What are you doing?" I recognized that voice. When I showed her the monitor she listened, but we both lost interest after a while.

Two weeks later I was pushing Blake in his stroller for a walk through the neighborhood, and I heard someone say, "Come on, Alex, get in the car." It was the same voice. I watched as a woman got her son into the car in their driveway. But I couldn't bring myself to tell her what I knew about her. And either the frequency changed or they stopped using their monitor, because we never heard from their house again.

A monitor is just one of the hundreds of gadgets and furnishings we consider necessary for having a baby in the house. I was scheduled to speak at a retreat in a little mountain town about two hours from home, and by the time we got the car seat, the stroller, the walker, the high chair, the fan to muffle noise, the portable bed, the tape player for his nighttime lullabies, the diapers, the suitcase, the baby food, and the toys in the car there was hardly enough room for the three of us. And this is all for one baby! No wonder parents on family vacations wear the same ugly shirt and shorts every day. There's no room for anything else once the kids are packed.

I had this vision of being the Jobes family in *The Grapes of Wrath*, or, more likely, the Clampetts in "The Beverly Hillbillies."

There are so many gadgets available to parents now that I wonder how my own parents got along without them. Or their parents. In some respects these things make parenting simpler. The walkers help children develop leg muscles and allows some mobility for the kids. Sometimes they allow too much mobility. One mom I know puts socks on her baby in the walker to cut down on the traction so the baby won't zoom too fast around the kitchen. High chairs keep the floors from becoming low-lying dumpsters. All this stuff is useful but not essential.

What is essential for parents is not the latest equipment, but the seriousness with which they accept their roles as dads and moms.

One of the women in my wife's office barely makes enough money to feed and clothe herself and her one-year-old daughter. They live in a two-room apartment over a liquor store in an unpleasant section of town. She has never considered buying the paraphernalia we have. A college friend lives in a small apartment above a theater in New York City, and she takes her children over the needle- and body-strewn sidewalks to Central Park every day so they have a place to play. What I might consider a necessity in parenting equipment is luxurious to these parents.

And they are still excellent parents. They love their children and have willingly made personal sacrifices for them. They love their spouses and have made a collective commitment that they will do what it takes to give their children a healthy home life. They have an atmosphere of love and acceptance to offer their children. I can't imagine how piles of equipment could improve on that.

Paul's counsel to Timothy's church is for us as parents too: "As for those who in the present age are rich, command them not to be haughty, or to set their hopes on the uncertainty of riches, but rather on God who richly provides us with everything for our enjoyment" (1 Tim. 6:17). That simplifies the focus for us, doesn't it?

Father, it is so easy to concentrate on what we can provide for our children. Remind us that our greatest provision is to point them, and us, to you.

Helping Create an Atmosphere

◆

Everyone who loves the parent loves the child.
1 John 5:1

Throughout history there has been a debate about who is the world's most influential person. Alexander the Great ranked up there for a while. Whatever pope is in office always gets a vote, as does the president of the United States. Before the break-up of the Soviet Union the leader of that region would be acknowledged. Hitler, Stalin, Peter the Great, Catherine the Great, Napoleon, Pete Rose, and others have been referred to as the most powerful people of their time. People of great wealth, like Malcolm Forbes, Armand Hammer, and Leona Helmsley, sometimes are front-runners, too.

But a person doesn't necessarily have to have an army or the Federal Reserve behind him to be thought of as powerful. When I was growing up, four young men from England named John, Paul, George, and Ringo were considered powerful, and they were feared by some people (like my parents) as much as Khrushchev.

For new parents, another influence is out there, and I believe he is more powerful than any of the others combined. His name is Fred Rogers. On his television show, "Mr. Rogers'

Neighborhood," he is the most soft-spoken, low-key person imaginable. And when I see the power he has over my son, who can barely sit up or grunt, yet who will sit still and stare at this mesmerizing monotone for the full thirty minutes, I realize that this is a powerful force indeed.

Unlike my parents' response to the Beatles, though, I like the fact that my son is getting messages from Fred Rogers. That's what makes the guy doubly powerful. Not only does he appear to talk directly to Blake, what he is saying is so positive that I *want* Blake to be influenced by him. He's not powerful because he's such a great orator. He's powerful because he's so calm and because he talks on a level children can understand. The power he has is willingly given to him by children and parents because he appears so trustworthy.

It's not too early for us as fathers to take an active role in choosing who will be our babies' primary influencers. When they go to school our choices will be more limited, so it makes sense to try to shape as much of the influence as is possible right now. One of our neighbors had a certain teenager take care of her baby until she found out that all the baby-sitter did was hold the baby in her lap while she watched MTV throughout the afternoon. Because more and more studies are revealing links between violent and other undesirable behaviors and hours spent watching sexist, stereotypical, and violent behaviors on television and in movies, the neighbor felt that she should try to exercise some control over what influenced her baby while she still had the chance.

A colleague who lived with his family in Cuba during the revolution told me how his three-year-old son was glued to the radio, listening to the reports of how Castro's new government was going to rid the country of the Anglos from the United States. The boy became terrified of what might become of his family, but he couldn't tear himself away from the radio.

The emotional scars of immersing himself for months with news of the terror have carried over into adulthood.

But actively providing a positive atmosphere involves more than making choices about television and radio. It involves choices about people. Who do we want to assist us in adjusting these new creatures to life on this planet? Besides us, who do we want to hold them for long periods of time? Who do we want to engage our children in play? Whose characters do we want to be common in our houses? Should we exercise some say in these areas?

A pastor told me that he has a practice of going into the church nursery every Sunday morning before the service and holding each baby for a minute or two. "It's a way of communicating to them that church is a good place, and there is comfort to be found there," he said. "It's an influence that communicates at the subconscious level."

I meet weekly with a group of men for breakfast—it's a tradition we have carried on for several years—and we go through a book together to grow spiritually as individuals and as a community. It has worked out naturally that we all are influences on one another's children because of this involvement in one another's lives. Sometimes our families get together for meals, sometimes we baby-sit one another's kids, sometimes we just have a few moments with them when we call or visit their dads. As we talked one morning about how grateful we were that our children were under the influence of one another, we decided that we wanted the influence to be more than a result of a chance encounter. We started looking for opportunities for one another's children to come into contact with us. We wanted people whose characters we believed in to be frequent visitors in our houses.

In the long run this may have little bearing on how our children turn out. They will make choices as they get older, and they may abandon the foundation that existed in their homes during the early years. But there is the chance that creating an atmosphere of positive influence will be valuable. I'm no psychologist, nor am I clairvoyant. But if I *can* have an impact in providing positive influences for my son, I should exercise that option regardless of what he *might* do with it later.

It is no accident that the people I want to be primary influences in Blake's life are believers in Christ, people whose lives have been changed by a Spirit of love and forgiveness. I don't think it is too early to communicate to Blake that faith in a living, personal God makes a difference in one's life. I'm trusting that he will remember this somehow, someday.

> *Heavenly Father, we know we can't control everything that influences our children, but we aren't totally powerless, either. Show us how your Spirit can be more influential in our homes.*

I've Got a Secret

◆

The Philistines are upon you, Samson!
Judges 16:20

In the story of Samson and Delilah, the Philistines knew that there must be an answer to the secret of Samson's strength. It wasn't his membership at the fitness club, they knew. He didn't exercise or even eat right. Yet he was the "Terminator" of his day, and his enemies wanted to find his weakness. He finally told his secret to Delilah (so his weakness was really *women*, not hair length), and the secret was used to destroy him.

Likewise, in George Orwell's book *1984*, Big Brother exploited the weakness of Winston Smith in order to destroy him. In the deepest recesses of his mind he feared rats. Somehow Big Brother knew this, so they had a bunch of rats attack him until he betrayed his partner and willfully worked for the corrupt government.

What application could this possibly have in a book about being a father? I believe my son has discovered my weakness and is using it to destroy me.

I can go without food. In fact, one of the spiritual disciplines I exercise is fasting, so skipping meals is not a big deal to me. I can go without bathing. As long as others don't need to be near me I can look and smell as bad as any boxcar rider without embarrassment. I can even go without reading, if forced.

But I must get a decent night's sleep.

Should Delilah visit me, she would only need to keep me from getting seven or eight hours of sleep for a couple of nights, and I would be tying animals' tails together and setting them on fire. If Big Brother wanted to unsettle me so much that I betrayed my partner and caved in to their perverse ways, they would only need to wake me up after four hours of sleep a few nights in a row. Somehow, Blake caught on to this.

We feel lucky if he sleeps three hours in a row at night before waking up hungry, irritable, dirty, with sore gums, or even playful. Marcia and I take turns getting up with him, which means each of us usually gets up twice each night. Sometimes we are up for just a few minutes, or, when he is in pain from teething, it can be for an hour. And then, as if my alarm is amused by our plight, it chooses to be loud and relentless in its reminder that the earth kept rotating regardless of how little time I spent in bed and that it is time to get ready for work.

I was trying to cram a full-time teaching job into three days a week so I could be all-day dad two days, while continuing some free-lance writing, consulting, and speaking. Marcia worked on the days I was home and in the evenings. The lack of sleep wore me down to a point where I didn't give some assignments at school because I knew I couldn't grade them. "This baby has been very good to us," one student told me. Tasks weren't getting completed. I was missing deadlines. Only the most pressing needs were getting attention. My face was getting puffy from lack of rest. I drank way too much coffee. I got crabbier by the minute. I even fainted in the shower after one very brief night—a result of too little sleep and too-hot water. I was losing control.

There wasn't even time to reflect on the kind of day it had been for the baby. The goal was to get through the day, and the slightest thing could throw off a delicately balanced schedule, which would cause the entire train to derail.

One encounter at about 2 A.M. scared me even more than the fainting incident. Blake was crying and Marcia's elbow told me it was my turn to take care of him. I thought that if I just walked with him and hummed a little I could settle him down quickly and not even notice the interruption in my sleep. But he wouldn't go along with it. He only got louder and more agitated. He yelled directly into my ear and dug his razor-sharp fingernails into my cheek. I set him in his bed on his back roughly—more roughly than I should have—and hissed a desperate "STOP IT!" The venom in my spirit scared him and me and we both burst into tears. I had momentarily lost my grip on things, and he knew it.

I picked him back up and we went into another room to see if I could redeem myself with him. Babies are amazing in this regard. Even when they are afraid of you they reach their arms out for you to hold them. Our dog does the same thing. I accidentally stepped on her paw, which caused her to shriek with pain. I turned to apologize, but before I could speak she jumped up and licked my hand, as if to say, "I know you didn't mean that. It's okay." That's how it seemed with Blake. As soon as I let my rage express itself he reached for me, as if to say, "I don't understand all of this, and apparently neither do you, but let's hold each other until we get calmed down." After about an hour he went back to sleep. I remained awake, fearful of what was happening.

For Marcia, the lack of sleep doesn't get to her as much as having the house a mess. Madness to her would be a room full of stuff out of place and being forbidden to put it away. I asked a colleague how she got everything done—her work, being a mom and a wife, keeping the house in order. Her response: "We live in a pigsty. When I start picking things up around the house, my three-year-old asks, 'Who's coming over?' " Big Brother could get to my wife with that one.

When a father feels insanity lurking over his shoulder, it is time to call for and accept help.

Our adult Sunday school class saw us derailing and did things like cook dinner for us a few times to get us back on track. It was difficult for me to accept their charity, but they convinced me that this was a common, brief stage that would pass into a much more joyful one. The fact that they were happy and alive, with children, helped persuade me.

> *Heavenly Father, there are times when I feel as if the world is exploiting my secret and is driving me mad. Help me to slow down, to enjoy the now, to acknowledge my need for others. Give me the trusting spirit of this baby.*

When More than *Your* World Changes

◆

When you send forth your spirit, they are created;
and you renew the face of the ground.
Psalm 104:30

How are things different when there is a new baby? In the family there is a radical change in focus. Partly because the baby demands it and partly because you simply want to, the baby's needs come first, and your own needs may not get met for some time. The only time I know that parents are encouraged to take care of their own needs first is in the preflight instructions on an airplane when the flight attendant says, in describing how to use the oxygen masks, to put your own mask on first, then assist your children. Otherwise the kids come first in almost all situations.

Parents sacrifice their own sleep so their kids can sleep longer. They delay making purchases like new clothes for themselves so that they can afford clothes for their kids. I'm not even tempted to buy myself a new pair of shoes because I saw what good shoes cost for babies just learning to walk.

But babies change more than the immediate family. Grandparents have a new focus for their lives, too. They have a new reason to go shopping. They stop strangers on the sidewalk or in checkout lines to tell them how funny or smart their grandkids are. We got a baseball bat with Blake's name etched into it because my mom saw one in someone's house with that person's grandkid's name on it. She pleaded with this guy to do one for Blake, telling him what tremendous athletic gifts Blake already has. The guy doesn't know me. But a zealous grandparent is a powerful force, and he complied.

Babies also change the people around us. It is as if the purity and innocence is so sacred that even coarse, gruff, profane people alter their behavior in the presence of a baby. Are they afraid of damaging this tiny psyche?

The couple next door have a sport fishing business. They are rough and they hang out with a rough group, and they weren't too fond of us as their neighbors. We didn't know they didn't like us, but we got the message when they mailed us a letter listing their grievances about our intrusion into their lives. This was no hand-delivered letter in our mailbox, either. Instead of giving it to us personally or talking it over with us, they mailed it.

You need to understand something about these people. They decided that their lawn was too much of a hassle to maintain. So they paved their backyard. It looked like an airport for miniature planes. They dumped gravel in the front yard and installed an irrigation system around the few bushes so they wouldn't have to water them personally.

They had no children, because, as they proudly proclaimed, "Kids would be such a pain."

Their front door has a homemade sign with a definition of solicitor on it, followed by a statement that anyone who was not invited to the house must be a solicitor, followed by the large, red-letter demand, "No Solicitors."

The note they sent was a list of violations we had committed against them as neighbors. Occasionally we had people over to our house who parked in front of our neighbor's place. They didn't like that. Occasionally I played my stereo too loudly and they heard it at their house. Our dog barked too much. Our trees bent over their fence on windy days and dropped leaves on their back runway. They wanted to know what we were going to do about these things. I proposed to my wife that we might consider sending a rattlesnake in the mail, but she overruled that.

We went to their house and discussed the problems, but there wasn't a lot I could do about the trees, I told them. Maybe they should write to God about that.

But then we got pregnant. I could tell that they were dreading this, because the bedrooms are on the side of the house that is near theirs, and they told us about the previous people in our house who had a baby and let him cry all day and night. Not so subtly, they told us what a pain it was to live next door to a new baby.

After we brought Blake home from the hospital, though, it was a different story. We invited them over to see him, and we insisted that they each hold him. Blake made all the right cooing sounds and wrinkled his face a lot and burrowed into each of them. He began changing them. They did what most normal adults do in the same situation. They talked baby talk to him, cooed back, and kissed him a lot. Then the husband asked something that showed what an immediate, radical change they had undergone in a matter of minutes.

"Do you think that, maybe when he is ten or so, he'd like to go fishing with me?" Marcia and I nearly fell over. Everyone had tears in their eyes by then because we all realized what was happening. The presence of a baby—pure and innocent—was changing the world around us. That Christmas they gave him a present—some play fishing equipment.

I can't explain what happened to our neighbors, or what happens to any of us when we come in contact with a baby. All I know is that we're different around them. We're happier, quieter, more trusting, more hopeful. Maybe we think that this little one means the human race will get a second chance, that there is hope for the future, that love is truly possible after all.

When I see these neighbors now, I don't view them with the same fear I once did, because they like my baby. They, like us, have had new life breathed in them.

> *Father in heaven, this new life in our home is creating several new lives. We are resurrecting. Thank you for the gift of new life through you and through your creation.*

Going Forward and Letting Go

◆

When Israel was a child, I loved him,
and out of Egypt I called my son.
The more I called them,
the more they went from me.
Hosea 11:1

There was no mistaking that this batting style was a God-given gift. The bat was straight up, just off his left shoulder, the wrists just loose enough to create the whip action in a fraction of a second, the feet were the perfect shoulder width apart, with knees slightly bent, the eyes were narrowed just enough to crowd out any distractions from making contact with the approaching ball. The pitcher's motion brought the batter's left foot forward slightly, the wrists whipped, the bat connected, and the ball went like a missile over everyone's head, amid the cheers of the crowd that had gathered.

We were at the beach, pushing Blake in his stroller along the packed sand, when we saw this batting demonstration. Like a scene out of the movie *The Natural*, everything the pitcher threw was sent screaming the other direction a moment later. The batter's facial expression never changed. After each hit he went back to his batting stance and focused on the next pitch.

"How old is the boy?" I hollered to the pitcher.

"Two," said his dad, winding up for another pitch. I positioned Blake's stroller so he could get a better view. I thought we were seeing a sneak preview of the next George Brett.

A couple of nights later Marcia and I were at a school banquet and, on the way home, decided to drop in at a coffee shop to see one of my students who worked there. The coffee shop isn't a traditional one like a Denny's. It's where the Punk subculture of San Diego hangs out—a clientele of Mohawk cuts, purple and orange hair, sizable pins in various fleshy parts of the face, and very loud music. I was in a suit and Marcia was in a very nice dress. Moments before at the banquet our appearance made us fit in. At the hangout we looked a bit out of place.

The student, who had become a close friend of ours, was on a break and didn't see us at first. We watched her sit at a table and stare into space. She was pale, gaunt, smoking her cigarette unconsciously, and looking like the most depressed person in the whole world.

Before I was a parent I probably would have written this scene off as a college kid trying to find her way, and figured that she would get through whatever this was. As a parent watching this scene, though, I was wounded. This was an establishment full of people who were looking for something. They might not know what they were looking for (do any of us?), but they ended up here.

I must confess that I am more comfortable with the thought of my son being an excellent baseball player than a punk-rocker with a rivet in his nose. But I must also confess that, at some point, I will have no say in what he ultimately does.

The author Alan Paton, in *Meditations for a Young Boy Confirmed* (Charles Scribner's Sons, 1954), writes:

> *I see my son is wearing long trousers, I tremble at this; I see he goes forward confidently, he does not know so fully his own gentleness.*

Go forward, eager and reverent child, see here I begin to take my hands away from you.

I shall see you walk careless on the edges of the precipice, but if you wish you shall hear no word come out of me.

What if Blake decides he doesn't value what Marcia and I value? His parents are both Christians. They both value education. What if Blake rejects nurturing his relationship with God? What if he drops out of school?

My whole soul will be sick with apprehension, but I shall not disobey you.

Life sees you coming, she sees you come with assurance towards her,

She lies in wait for you; she cannot but hurt you;

Marcia and I talked about what we could do now to help Blake avoid doing what we witnessed at that coffee shop. It was a frustrating discussion because we knew that whatever happened would be Blake's choice, not ours. We can't cause the good decisions or stop the bad ones. We can't create life's joys for him later on or protect him from life's crushing blows.

Go forward, go forward, I hold the bandages and ointments ready,

And if you would go elsewhere and lie alone with your wounds, why I shall not intrude upon you,

If you would seek the help of some other person, I shall not come forcing myself upon you.

If you should fall into sin, innocent one, that is the way of this pilgrimage;

Struggle against it, not for one fraction of a moment concede its dominion.

It will occasion you grief and sorrow, it will torment you,

But hate not God, nor turn from Him in shame or self-reproach;

He has seen many such, His compassion is as great as His Creation.

Be tempted and fall and return, return and be tempted and fall

A thousand times and a thousand, even to a thousand thousand.

For out of this tribulation there comes a peace, deep in the soul, and surer than any dream.

I remember when I decided to leave the business world to teach and write. My dad, a businessman, didn't understand it and opposed it. He wasn't heavy-handed, but he was disappointed. Our relationship didn't change because of it, though. I remember when I made some life-style choices that I believe God opposed. I was tempted, fell, and returned. "His compassion was as great as His Creation."

I am preparing the bandages and ointments for when Blake makes his decisions. But the bandages and ointments will be for both of us, because we will bruise and bleed together, as my father did for me, and as our heavenly Father continues to do for his entire creation.

Go forward, children. Go forward Blake. Go forward.

Father, thank you for bleeding for and with your creation. Show us when to hold the bandages and ointments ready. Show us how to give the future to you.

The Future of Civilization

◆

I am like an evergreen cypress;
your faithfulness comes from me.
Hosea 14:8

Every adult generation has worried about the generation to come. Socrates spoke in the 3rd century B.C. about how the young people of Greece were destined for failure because they had no respect for authority or their elders. Twenty-two centuries later in this country there was fear and trembling over young people caught up in comic books, Elvis, rock and roll, and television. Remember the Broadway show *The Music Man*? Remember the gasps from parents when Robert Preston mentioned finding kids reading dime novels, having nicotine stains on their fingers, and playing pool? He convinced River City that "Oh, we've got Trouble with a capital T and that rhymes with P and that stands for Pool!" Surely the youth of River City were doomed.

We've all heard the stories about how television would not show Elvis from the waist down because his movements might corrupt our youth. More than once in my younger years I heard the Beatles likened to Hitler's Nazis, because of their "murderous effects" on young minds. The current addiction to television and video games prompted one social critic to call today's children "Vidiots."

For the most part, though, society has endured the potential problems and become hopeful that the coming generation might be able to improve things. Today's young people could be the ones capable of solving pollution problems, economic crises, racial conflicts. At least that hope has usually emerged.

But there is also good reason to be more concerned about the generation to come than other generations were. Every generation has had a version of playground fights. I got in one and needed several stitches to close the gash over my eye. Every generation has experienced groups claiming that a certain area was their "turf." But those previous generations weren't carrying guns. The fight I got into as a kid, if it were to occur today, would likely end in a death, probably mine. And turf-protection exercises today are gun battles that include random drive-by shootings. It isn't rougher just in the inner cities, either. In the former havens of suburbs and rural areas, the once-safe landscape has changed dramatically.

Even with a reduced threat of nuclear war between superpower nations, this is an increasingly dangerous world in which our babies are growing up. *Fortune* magazine published an article on August 10, 1992, called "Struggling to Save Our Kids," and it made me shudder as a parent.

Consider: The parents of 2,750 children separate or divorce each day in the United States. More than half of all white children and three-quarters of all black children will spend part of their childhood in a single-parent household. About 90 kids a day are taken from their parents and put into an overcrowded foster care system. More than three children per day die at the hands of their abusive parents. More than one million latchkey children, ages five to fourteen, take care of themselves for much of the day. The typical fourteen-year-old does one hour of homework per day and watches three hours of television. More than 2,200 kids drop out of school every day.

More than 1,400 teenage girls per day become mothers. Homicide by firearms is the leading cause of death for black teenagers and the third leading cause for whites, after car accidents and suicide. Every day more than 500 children ages ten to fourteen begin using illegal drugs, and more than 1,000 start drinking alcohol. The fastest growing segment of the labor force is mothers of children under six, representing more than eleven million children who need day care.

The millions of young people described here will be our replacements, if they survive. They are the ones our babies will be growing up with. They are our children. I realize that part of what it means to be a parent is to worry, but I'm more than worried about what's ahead. I'm frightened. What will it take to save our children from continued destruction?

"Only healthy families headed by responsible parents in caring communities can succeed in raising healthy kids," said former U.S. Education Secretary William Bennett in the *Fortune* article.

No doubt everyone has a different definition of what a healthy family is and what responsible parents are, but we all can at least make a commitment to our children and communities that we will spend our lives trying to break the cycle that is currently spinning out of control.

"If the well-being of its children is the proper measure of the health of a civilization, the United States is in grave danger," writes Louis Richman, the *Fortune* article's reporter.

Can we help? I believe the answer lies in our response to Hosea 14:1: "Return, O Israel, to the LORD your God; for you have stumbled because of your iniquity." We may need to get politically active, lobby government, participate in neighborhood groups, join the PTA, become foster parents, get more involved in our local churches. But we also need to approach our heavenly Father for direction in being healthy, responsible parents who can have an impact on our communities.

In return, God promises,

> *I will love them freely,*
> *for my anger has turned from them.*
> *I will be like the dew to Israel;*
> *he shall blossom like the lily. . . .*
> *[Israel] shall again live beneath my shadow. . . .*
> *It is I who answer and look after you (Hosea 14:4-8).*

As Christian parents we can love God, model him to our families and communities, and be participants in saving this generation by being obedient to the direction he gives us. It is too late to do nothing.

> *Father, we want our children to grow up in a safer, more pleasant world than the one they see today. Show us how we can be your hands and feet to make a difference.*

Changed Forever

◆

God saw everything that he had made,
and indeed, it was very good.
Genesis 1:31

At the one-year point both for our baby to be on this planet and for us to wallow through parenting, I believe I have babies figured out. That's right, I'm an expert, and I'm going to start my own radio program. I'll have lots of guests to impress my listeners with my contacts, and there probably will be an offer to develop something for cable television.

But it will be a very short program, because it is an unbelievably simple concept. The key to understanding babies is this: Babies only want what adults want. Our desires don't change as we grow up. Isn't that simple? It's true.

For instance, we all want dry pants. I was in Australia a few years ago and had only one pair of jeans with me. Somehow they got dirty, so I went to a laundry and washed them. I didn't leave them in the dryer long enough, though, because when I put them back on, they were damp. No problem, I thought. They'll dry out as I wear them. They did, eventually, but at the expense of my skin underneath. I developed a nasty rash that took several days to heal. It was extremely uncomfortable, and, had it been socially acceptable, I would have cried in protest. That's what babies do. They protest wet and dirty pants.

They also protest when their stomachs are empty. So do we. How many times in our lives have we uttered this preposterous phrase, "I'm starving!" Of course we're not. And neither are our babies when they cry out for food. But what we're all really saying is, "This empty feeling in my stomach is uncomfortable, and it is making me irritable. Would the responsible party please fix the problem?" I went on a three-day fast while camping out with a college friend as part of a Native American history class project. Now *that* was uncomfortable. All I could think about was how uncomfortable I was. I even dreamed about food. For the first two days my entire being cried out for food. But I lived through it.

Sometimes babies cry for no apparent reason, yet they calm down if someone picks them up. Are there adults on this planet who, when distressed by legitimate or other reasons, wouldn't feel better if someone would hold them, sing to them, or kiss them softly about their faces? When Blake flies into a rage, he wants to be held tightly and convinced that someone is taking his problem seriously. Don't we all want that? Isn't that the antidote for all rage, no matter how old we are?

Wasn't that the key to David Wilkerson's success in *The Cross and the Switchblade*? Isn't that what we need from our heavenly Father, to know that he is there, taking us seriously? Isn't that also what we need from each other? Isn't that what keeps spouses together? Isn't that what keeps the world together? There is no feeling comparable to two people hugging one another. Babies know this. They cry out for it.

There is one more thing babies want that we all want. They want to feel that they are not alone. If we put Blake in the middle of the floor and give him several books to look at, he is generally content. But if he sees that we have left him in the room by himself, he lets out a wail that would break a heart of stone. If we give him the books and stay in the room, not even talking to him, he's fine. Adults are often like that. While it feels good to get away from human contact for a while, there is also a yearning to feel that we are a part of something. That's the secret to the Rotary Club. When you're out of town and have to miss a meeting, then, by George, you find a meeting in the town you're in and you attend. It makes you feel that you're involved in something bigger than yourself. We need that as adults. So do babies.

We are approaching the end of this first year with a variety of feelings. For instance, we are very tired. Maybe by this time next year we will either have figured out a way to accommodate the desires and needs of all three of us, or two of us will have lowered our expectations. But fatigue isn't the dominant feeling right now. Gratitude is. I still can't believe how blessed we feel by this fun, friendly, funny little boy. We want the world to stop on his birthday, as we believe it did when he was born. That this helpless, trusting, needy, loving bead of life was given to our care is a humbling experience. We have a big party planned for him that will probably wear him out and make him sick. It's the adult way of celebrating.

In addition to gratitude we are still awestruck. The chasm from witnessing birth to witnessing first steps is vast, but we've seen it with our own eyes. Our wonder multiplies with each new sound or movement or indication that the baby is catching on. For parents the wonder is more than just getting to experience childhood again. The wonder lies in being witnesses to a being who is experiencing things for the first time—things that for us are routine. We are reminded of what a marvelous experience it is to be alive.

As we approach the end of this first year, the inevitable question must be: Are we interested in going through this again? Could another baby possibly be this wonderful? Would those same feelings of wonder be as intense for a second baby as they were for the first? Are we ready for the anxiety, for the feeling of being overwhelmed, for the terror of the unfinished tasks? Will two little ones double all of the above feelings?

I don't have to think very hard about this, to be honest. I might need another year or so to regroup, but I like being a dad. Bring them on.

Father, you participate every moment with your creation, and you take such delight in it. Thank you for giving us a glimpse of your joy by making us parents. We delight in these good gifts. Because of them we will never be the same.

Blake C. Nelson's version of life with dad, drawn at age 6.